T0316584

Cambridge Elements ≡

Elements in Ancient Egypt in Context
edited by
Gianluca Miniaci
University of Pisa
Juan Carlos Moreno García
CNRS, Paris
Anna Stevens
University of Cambridge and Monash University

SEEING PERFECTION

Ancient Egyptian Images beyond Representation

Rune Nyord
Emory University

CAMBRIDGE
UNIVERSITY PRESS

CAMBRIDGE
UNIVERSITY PRESS

University Printing House, Cambridge CB2 8BS, United Kingdom

One Liberty Plaza, 20th Floor, New York, NY 10006, USA

477 Williamstown Road, Port Melbourne, VIC 3207, Australia

314–321, 3rd Floor, Plot 3, Splendor Forum, Jasola District Centre,
New Delhi – 110025, India

79 Anson Road, #06–04/06, Singapore 079906

Cambridge University Press is part of the University of Cambridge.

It furthers the University's mission by disseminating knowledge in the pursuit of education, learning, and research at the highest international levels of excellence.

www.cambridge.org
Information on this title: www.cambridge.org/9781108744140
DOI: 10.1017/9781108881494

First published 2020

A catalogue record for this publication is available from the British Library.

ISBN 978-1-108-74414-0 Paperback
ISSN 2516-4813 (online)
ISSN 2516-4805 (print)

Seeing Perfection

Ancient Egyptian Images beyond Representation

Elements in Ancient Egypt in Context

DOI: 10.1017/9781108881494
First published online: October 2020

Rune Nyord
Emory University

Author for correspondence: rune.nyord@emory.edu

Abstract: This Element offers a new approach to ancient Egyptian images informed by interdisciplinary work in archaeology, anthropology, and art history. Sidestepping traditional perspectives on Egyptian art, the Element focuses squarely on the ontological status of the image in ancient thought and experience. To accomplish this, Section 2 takes up a number of central Egyptian terms for images, showing that a close examination of their etymology and usage can help resolve long-standing questions on Egyptian imaging practices. Section 3 discusses ancient Egyptian experiences of materials and manufacturing processes, while Section 4 categorizes and discusses the different purposes and functions for which images were created. The Element as a whole thus offers a concise introduction to ancient Egyptian imaging practices for an interdisciplinary readership, while at the same introducing new ways of thinking about familiar material for the Egyptological reader.

Keywords: ancient Egypt, ancient Egyptian art, ancient Egyptian religion, statue, image

ISBNs: 9781108744140 (PB), 9781108881494 (OC)
ISSNs: 2516-4813 (online), ISSN 2516-4805 (print)

Contents

1 Introduction

What was an image to the ancient Egyptians? This is the simple, yet many-faceted, central question posed by the present Element. In attempting to answer this question, it eschews a strong tradition in Egyptology of interpreting uses of images with reference to beliefs in magic and possession by souls. Such explanatory models tend in practice to shut down interpretation, as it is difficult to go any further than positing a particular belief on the part of the Egyptians. They also often end up resting on speculative foundations, as Egyptian texts, images, and practices were very rarely interested in expounding dogma of the kind such an approach aims to reconstruct.

In reaction to this tradition, part of the move in this work is rhetorical as an attempt to 'take seriously' (cf. Nyord 2018b) what the ancient Egyptians thought and did. In so doing, however, the approach espoused here opens up a number of new avenues that tend to be closed off by the traditional focus on beliefs. How does the image relate to that which it depicts, if it is not possessed by a soul? And what would be the more fundamental entailments of living in a world in which such connections exist? While far from answering all such questions definitively, the Element at least sketches how such questions might be formulated in practice, and how we can avoid familiar pitfalls in attempting to answer them.

Modern perspectives have tended to focus our attention on Egyptian images as something that needs to be decoded or deciphered, an approach partly justified by the close connections between image and writing in ancient Egypt (e.g. Tefnin 1984). However, recent thinking about images more generally has tended to stress that this approach is just one of two overall modes in which images can be experienced. In the influential formulation of medieval art historian Hans Belting (1994), images can be approached as either 'likeness' or 'presence'. The former approach takes the image as something which, in mimicking the appearance of what it depicts, reminds the viewer of the depicted entity or – once decoded – makes a statement about it. As 'presence', the image becomes a manifestation or concretion of what it depicts, allowing it to be encountered in a particular time, place, and manner. In the words of Mitchell (2005), the former approach corresponds to an interest in what an image *means*, while the latter focuses instead on what the image *does* (cf. Sansi 2013: 18–20).

Egyptological approaches to Egyptian images have drawn on both approaches, albeit somewhat selectively. Because of the close entanglement between image and writing alluded to previously, the act of decoding by identifying iconographic elements has been, and still is, an important corner-stone of understanding ancient Egyptian images. On the other hand, the question of what an image *does* has tended to be approached by more or less inventive ascriptions of particular beliefs to the ancient Egyptians concerning the images. Typically, such beliefs will concern the 'magical' properties of images – how (the Egyptians believed) they could come to life when not watched, how they could serve as habitat for one or more Egyptian souls, etc. In a more theorized form, such functions have been labelled as 'performative' (e.g. Sweeney 2004: 67), sometimes explicitly paralleling them with linguistic 'speech acts' which establish the reality of that which they express (e.g. Assmann 2015).

However, it is useful to turn this traditional formulation of the problem on its head. Rather than asking what the Egyptians must have believed to make them treat images very differently from our expectations, it is helpful to consider our own intuitions about images, especially because these intuitions turn out to be something of a special case in the broader perspective of global art history. Often labeled 'representationalism' (e.g. Bolt 2004; Barad 2007: 46–50), or simply a concept of 'representation' (e.g. Espirito Santo and Tassi 2013), these intuitions and expectations rest on a set of fundamental assumptions about the world widespread in modern Western culture, but much less prevalent elsewhere.

To put it briefly, representationalism posits a specific understanding of the relationship between an image and the entity or object which it depicts. Most notably, the only connection between image and entity is a mental one, in the mind of the maker of the image and/or the minds of the audience. This can be accomplished through mimicking visual aspects (mimesis), through an established set of signs or symbols (iconography), or through other conventions (typically an inscribed identification). However, none of this entails any real-world connection between image and entity, and the two lead completely separate lives despite any mental associations they may elicit. A change in the image will not affect the object in any way, nor will a change in the object have any influence on the image. A corollary of this relationship is that the depicted object enjoys a primacy not accorded to the image. The image is a mere copy, since its appearance is dependent on that of the object, while the inverse is not true.

As can be seen from this brief characterization, the representationalist understanding of images rests fundamentally on a distinction between the mental and the physical. Imagery is solely a matter of mental representation, while in physical terms an image is a distinct object subjected to laws of causality like any other. The analogy to the relationship between a linguistic message and the medium in which it is communicated is clear. This distinction between the mental and the physical is often referred to as 'Cartesian dualism' after its most prominent proponent in Western philosophy, René Descartes (1596–1650). Intuitive as it is to those who have been brought up with it, it is nonetheless fraught with problems. This is true in relation to its internal logic where it is difficult to explain, for example, how the physical and the mental can interact in sensory perception or will-based agency, if they are completely separate and incommensurable realms as Cartesianism posits. But a more practical problem arises if this relatively parochial (in the sense of being characteristic of a particular segment of Western cultural history) set of assumptions are raised to universal principles and used as the basis for understanding other cultures that did not share them (cf. Nyord 2009: 35–44, and the closely comparable case of ancient Near Eastern art in Bahrani 2003).

Thus, rather than granting representationalism logical primacy by asking what the Egyptians must have believed to make them disregard its tenets, this work suggests a different approach. While agreeing with representationalism that images are fundamentally about relationships between an object and that which it depicts, this relationship is not regarded by necessity as a representational one along the lines sketched previously. Rather, the exact nature of the relationship needs to be deduced from what the Egyptian did with and said about the image (cf. Henare, Holbraad, and Wastell 2007). In particular, as will be seen in the following sections, the Egyptians tended to assume close, intrinsic connections between images and that which they depict, in Gadamer's words an 'ontological communion' (Gadamer 2004 [1960]: 137). In what follows, we will broaden this idea considerably and, expressed programmatically, this work will posit that we attain a better understanding of Egyptian images by following a simple fundamental principle: What appears to us intuitively as relations of representation (mimesis, symbolism, etc.), can more fruitfully be regarded as ontological connections. Importantly, this is not an ascription of a particular belief to the Egyptians (as we will see, this basic principle can lead in very different, sometimes opposite directions), but rather, it is a broadening of the interpretive field by sidestepping a specific 'belief' of our own.

On a smaller scale, such an approach also serves to remedy one of the key points of criticism against traditional Egyptological approaches to ancient Egyptian art, namely the tendency to decontextualize artworks to study them according to purely iconographic and stylistic criteria (e.g. Verbovsek 2005; Widmaier 2017). By making the words and actions of the Egyptians the main criterion for determining even the fundamental ontological status of the image, we can avoid bracketing the cultural context out of the act of interpretation.

1.1 Ontology of the Image

Central for the questions taken up in this Element is the ontology of the image: What is an image fundamentally, what is its relationship to what it depicts, and what can an image do? Ontology has become a popular topic in recent years under such headings as speculative realism and new materialism (e.g. Harman 2018; Bennett 2010; Barad 2007), which have, in some cases, provided entirely new conceptual frameworks for thinking about modes of being. It is worth stressing here that the aim of the present Element is relatively modest in comparison. Although any ontological analysis must necessarily make use of the concepts and vocabulary available to the scholar, I am interested here primarily in exploring what an image was *for the Egyptians*. To that end, I have resorted in several instances to ancient Egyptian terminology in order to complement established philosophical and art historical vocabulary. As aptly stated by anthropologists Henare, Holbraad, and Wastell, the kind of analysis undertaken here 'has little to do with trying to determine how other people think about the world. It has to do with how *we* must think in order to conceive a world the way they do' (Henare, Holbraad, and Wastell 2007: 15). This method of adjusting our own concepts until the statements and practices of the people studied make sense lies behind the move suggested of abandoning representationalism from the outset. As such, it is broadly aligned with the method recently suggested by art historian James Elkins for 'world art studies' of 'employing indigenous texts as interpretive languages' (Elkins 2008: 113), although the 'ontological turn' in anthropology would purport to go significantly further than an art historical interpretation. On the other hand, such an approach goes in a different direction than more conventional ideas along the lines that that the 'special ontological status' of religious images is 'tied to the belief of their devotees' (Belting 2016: 235), in which the image itself can be neatly separated from the irrational ideas its makers and users may have held about it (see Needham 1972 for an anthropological critique of the concept of 'belief').

·Another, partly unrelated (cf. Latour 2009), recent use of the notion of ontology is worth mentioning here as well. In anthropologist Philippe Descola's monumental *Beyond Nature and Culture* (Descola 2013 [2005]; cf. also Descola 2010), he proposes an overall quadripartite scheme of ontologies, which aims, in principle, to capture worldviews of all human cultures. The scheme is based on the interrelationship members of a given society experience between 'interiority' (the identity, agency, and experience of sentient beings) and 'exteriority' (types of bodies and bodily capacities). Ancient Egypt falls relatively clearly under Descola's heading of 'analogism', an ontological scheme characterized by the living creatures of the cosmos being interrelated through small incremental differences in terms of both interiority and exteriority (Descola 2013 [2005]: 201–31, cf. Quirke 2015: 39–40, and Brémont 2018 for examples of the employment of this idea in Egyptology; and a set of similar 'analogistic' features *avant la lettre* listed in Finnestad 1989: 30–3). This mode of experiencing the world with multiple hidden interconnections of homology and contrast often finds expression in widespread correlations between microcosm and macrocosm, found, for example, in practices of healing and divination, and indeed mythological concepts are often used in Egypt to establish connections of this kind (Nyord 2018a).

Of direct relevance to the topic of this Element, analogical ontologies also tend to imply certain specific conceptions and practices relating to images (Descola 2010: 163–213). One striking effect of the myriad analogical connections between different beings is the conception of chimeric creatures combining and interchanging clearly identifiable body parts from different species. Ancient Egypt is famous for its animal-headed gods, sphinxes, and other composite beings (cf. Wengrow 2014), a phenomenon that would indicate, in Descola's scheme, the presence of underlying connections and analogies between the different kinds of living beings.

Another effect of the attention to sometimes-interchangeable parts and their role in a whole is a widespread use of collections and configurations of individual images. Not unlike the individual chimera, such assemblages are capable of functioning as a united whole despite being made up clearly heterogeneous elements, the configuration and interrelationships between which in turn elicit the function of the whole. In Egypt, such assemblages are constituted, for example, by heavily laden tables with different offerings (Robins 1998), the combined worship of a group of different gods housed in the same temple but each in their own shrine (e.g. David 2018: 125–82), or, perhaps most saliently, in collections of grave goods, many of which are clearly imagistic, deposited in tomb chambers around the body of the deceased (e.g. Grajetzki 2003).

As will be seen throughout this work, this expectation correctly predicts an overall concern with the capacity of images to establish connections and relationships, first and foremost between the image and that which it depicts, but often images form much more complex networks of connections, potentially incorporating multiple different images, materials, elements of iconography, etc. For reasons that will gradually become clear through the subsequent discussion, it is often a moot point whether such assemblages illustrate already-existing connections, or whether they establish and elicit new connections through their material configuration. Either way, the assemblage allows the whole to become manifest in a given time, place, and manner through the presence and configuration of the images constituting its parts.

In what follows, the word 'power' will be used to designate this kind of dynamic, but hidden, connection which has the capacity to channel or guide observable processes, especially the ways in which beings like gods and ancestors become manifest. The Egyptians had several different concepts designating such capacities, though in many cases we have no way of knowing which particular category an Egyptian would have used. This is why a general etic term like 'power' is often preferable.

The expectations for ancient Egyptian imaging practices arising from Descola's framework indicate the importance of concepts such as relationality and assemblages, and these ideas have been theorized independently of this framework in recent archaeology (e.g. Alberti 2016; Harris 2017a; Harrison-Buck and Hendon 2018). In particular, the notion of affect plays an important role in the understanding of images espoused here. The notion is used here primarily in its philosophical sense of 'capacity to affect and be affected' (cf. Pellini 2018: 46) rather than the everyday use to designate charged emotional states (although the two are sometimes combined with varying results in recent scholarship, e.g. Harris 2017b and the discussion in Pellini 2018: 45–7). The importance of the concept for interpreting ancient Egyptian images is that it allows us to conceptualize the Egyptians' own practices where images are used to establish relations of mutual influence between the depiction, the depicted, and other places, entities, and powers.

A general Egyptian concept of particular relevance in this regard is what could be termed the 'emergence principle' (Fig. 1). Across a number of different myths, rituals, and other practices, a shared idea is that of creation and becoming as a process of differentiation. More specifically, that which is created, be it a baby, the sun, the sprouting grain, the landscape returning to normal when the Nile flood recedes, or the glazing of a ceramic vessel, is hidden in an unseen state of potential existence inside a 'container' from which it has not yet become distinguishable. The process of becoming is then experienced as an emergence from this undifferentiated material by turning into a distinct entity. This emergence principle is useful for understanding a wide range of concepts and practices in ancient Egypt, and especially for seeing the connection between instantiations of different order, such as mythological narratives and concrete images.

1.2 About This Element

This volume deliberately addresses a diverse readership. The general reader will find here an introduction, with numerous central examples, to what the

Fig. 1 A striking example of the emergence principle in Egyptian thought and experience: A 'corn-mummy' consisting of grain and earth wrapped in linen and coated with resin, and embodying the hidden creative power associated with the god Osiris. Michael C. Carlos Museum, 2018.10.1C. Photo courtesy of the Georges Ricard Foundation and the California Institute of World Archaeology.

Egyptians did with images. It is not intended as a general history of Egyptian art, but rather takes a case-study-based approach in which image practices are classified and interpreted, without comprehensively covering such traditional areas as iconography or stylistic development. In this sense, this Element is complementary to art historical overviews (with Robins 2008 as an excellent and readily available example), and the complete newcomer to Egyptian art history may fruitfully read it in tandem with such works.

The advanced student or professional practitioner of Egyptology will be familiar with much of the material discussed in the case studies, but will find new perspectives on this well-known material. A number of traditional ideas in Egyptological scholarship are taken up for discussion and re-evaluation, often in the light of concepts and approaches developed in neighbouring fields. In some cases, this leads to posing entirely different sets of questions from the concerns traditionally associated with particular bodies of material. For this readership, the Element is thus meant not merely as a convenient collection of phenomena not previously discussed as a whole, but also as an invitation to engage with old material in new ways, with many of the analyses presented here raising questions of relevance well beyond the case studies chosen to illustrate them.

Scholars from neighbouring, more general, fields (e.g. archaeology, art history, anthropology) will not only find the overview and classification of Egyptian image practices already mentioned, but will also see them approached through questions and concepts likely to be more relevant to them than many traditional treatments of Egyptian art and religion. The aim is to show that, far from being an exceptional area of archaeology or art history, Egyptian images are amenable to similar perspectives to those under development in other parts of those fields, and with a mostly unexplored capacity for bringing new concepts and materials to such theoretical discussions. The Element thus also constitutes an invitation to this group of readers to engage with the perspectives offered by Egyptian image practices in thinking about such current topics as affect, relationality, functions of images and visuality, and beyond.

The diverse readership and modest size of this volume mean that each of these aspects can only be explored relatively briefly, and many of the analyses presented here could be readily expanded upon along the lines suggested here. Rather than completeness, in most cases the discussion here aims instead at providing an introduction to each phenomenon along with a methodological (and in some cases theoretical) orientation arguing ways in which it can fruitfully be viewed, along with some central, recent references as a way further into the topic. The recurring use of the word 'invitation' in the preceding paragraphs is thus no accident: First and foremost this work is meant to provide inspiration for future thinking about Egyptian images by opening this material up to multiple, and in many cases Egyptologically speaking new, perspectives.

As a starting point for the exploration of uses of ancient Egyptian images, Section 2 takes up a number of central ancient terms and concepts for images. Several of the words used by the Egyptians to refer to images reveal aspects of their thought and experiences, especially concerning the pivotal question of the relationship between the image and that of which it is an image. At the end of the section, two influential Egyptological hypotheses about Egyptian images are examined, namely those explaining images as material substrates for the soul-like concepts of *ka* and *ba* respectively. Both of these are found to be problematical, and the section ends with a general discussion of how the ontology of ancient Egyptian images may be understood.

Section 3 broadens the perspective by moving from the concepts of images themselves to the material and social contexts in which images were created and received. Of relevance here is not just the social roles and positions of artists and patrons, but also questions of how the ontology of the image outlined in the previous section can be squared with traditional categories such as uses and choices of materials, the aesthetic dimension of images, and other 'design choices' such as posture and iconography.

Finally, Section 4 looks at the practical uses of ancient Egyptian images. Based on a rough typology of potential effects of the image, the section discusses not only the pervasive idea of the image as the material presence of the depicted entity, but also ways of modifying this basic scheme to put emphasis on relationality, causing change, and the ability of the image to function as substitute. The last part of this section discusses reasons for, and effects of, subsequent damaging or changing of images.

2 Image Terminology

An important step towards an understanding of Egyptian conceptions and experiences of images can be taken by examining the ways in which the Egyptians categorized and discussed images (Ockinga 1984; Schulz 1992: 700–20; Eschweiler 1994; Hoffmann 2001; Eaton 2007). Ancient Egyptian language had a number of different terms for what we would term images, some of which could also be used to designate phenomena to which we would not apply this label. By examining the etymology and usage of some of the most important Egyptian terms, we can get a number of pointers regarding the main question that was identified in the Introduction, namely that of the nature of the relationship between an image and that which it depicts.

It is worth noting from the outset that these terms show a great deal of overlap in their actual usage (i.e. regarding what kind of images they can be used to refer to). Thus, most of them can be used of images in both two and three dimensions, and with very few exceptions noted in the following, they are not generally restricted to specific categories such as individual genres of sculpture. Thus, rather than being a catalogue of different kinds of Egyptian images, the examination of terminology demonstrates the different designations used by the Egyptians to characterize the roles of images, especially concerning their relationship to what they depict. For this reason, the following discussion is focused on a smaller subset of ancient Egyptian image designations, where the etymology and usage of the terms offer insights into the underlying conceptions of images.

2.1 Mimesis and Idealization: The Concept of *twt*

One of the oldest and most frequent ancient Egyptian designations of images in two and three dimensions is the word *twt*, derived from a root usually translated as meaning 'to be like, to resemble' (Fig. 2). The notion that an image is supposed to resemble that which it represents, and that the image can correspondingly be designated as a 'likeness', is very familiar to modern observers. Perhaps this is the reason why the semantics of this image concept has rarely

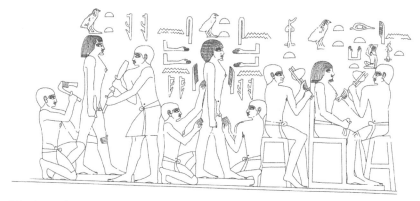

Fig. 2 Tomb relief of *twt*-statues in the making. The tomb of Ti (Saqqara). Drawn by Henrijette Vex Nyord after Wild 1966: Pl. CLXXIII.

attracted further attention. However, it is clear to even the casual observer of ancient Egyptian art that simple mimesis – an attempt to capture as faithfully as possible the visual details of what is represented – is rarely the predominant aim in itself. Rather, this aim is significantly tempered by tendencies towards idealization and of depiction according to preexisting archetypes (Laboury 2010). For example, human bodies tend to be proportioned according to set canons, rather than representing specific body types or bodily features (Robins 1994), and depictions of private people often assimilate their facial features to those of the reigning king (Jørgensen 2015). This raises the question in what sense Egyptian images were regarded as 'likenesses' as implied by the use of the term *twt*.

A pivotal example of what the Egyptians meant by the root *twt* comes from the inscription on an obelisk still standing in the Karnak temple where it was erected by the female pharaoh Hatshepsut (r. 1473–1458 BCE) (Fig. 3). The obelisk was part of a pair dedicated to the god Amun and Hatshepsut's father, King Thutmose I. The inscription details the impressive feat of manufacturing the enormous (almost 30 metres high) monolithic obelisks, which were originally covered with large quantities of gold foil, and in particular it stresses the special relationship between Hatshepsut and Amun which motivated the creation of the monuments. Towards the end of the inscription on the base of the obelisk, Hatshepsut presents some considerations of how the obelisks would be viewed by posterity, stating '*He who hears this shall not say that what I have related is boasting; but rather say "How it resembles (twt) her!"'* (*Urk.* IV, 368, 3–5).

The opposition between boasting and correspondence with reality is immediately understandable, but there is one detail in the passage that is surprising.

Fig. 3 Granite statue of Hatshepsut kneeling by the processional route of Amun leading to the shrine in her mortuary temple. Metropolitan Museum of Art, 29.3.1.

Instead of the expected correspondence between the description and what actually happened, the passage instead emphasizes the correspondence between the description and the person: 'How it resembles (*twt*) *her!*'

The expression 'How it resembles' was already old in the fifteenth century BCE, and an occurrence several centuries earlier can help us shed light on the way Hatshepsut uses it. Thus, in a context which is unfortunately not preserved, the Middle Egyptian wisdom text called *The Teaching of Sasobek* reads, '"How it resembles (*twt*) him!" is what people say of the one who has acted according to his propensity (*sḥrw*)' (Barns 1956: pl. 2, B1, 10). Here we find the notion of resemblance expressed as a direct connection between the behaviour of a human being on the one hand and his 'propensity' on the other. We will encounter the concept of *sḥrw*, 'tendency, propensity' again as an expression of the characteristic pattern which a being or phenomenon follows. Thus, in the *Teaching of Sasobek*, it is the behaviour of a human being which 'resembles' the person exactly in so far as the behaviour is in accordance with the person's hidden nature. A more apposite translation in such cases might thus be something along the lines of 'characteristic' or 'typical'.

In light of this use of the expression, Hatshepsut's inscription can be understood as entailing more than just a claim of veracity. In using the expression 'How it resembles!', she is not so much stressing the accuracy of the technical description, but rather affirming that the presented relationship to the god Amun is in accordance with her 'nature'. In fact, the text following the quoted passage deals precisely with this aspect in some detail.

Against this background, the apparent paradox between images as 'something which resembles', on the one hand, and the various Egyptian image practices that go strongly against a mimetic ideal, on the other, begins to dissolve, as it turns out to be heavily dependent on our representationalist intuitions about what 'resembling' entails. As has been seen, the Egyptian notion of *twt* does not refer to a mimetic copying of a visual impression. Rather, the idea of 'resemblance' refers to a correspondence with a deeper nature (such as Hatshepsut's divine origin) or the defining features that make one a member of a particular category. As will be seen throughout this work, this notion of 'resemblance' can explain a number of peculiarities of Egyptian image practices (cf., for example, the question of whether Egyptian sculpture can be regarded as 'portraits', e.g. Spanel 1988; Laboury 2010).

2.2 The Image as Guide: The Concept of *sšmw*

The word *sšmw* is used to denote a wide range of images, generally of a ritual nature, from cult statues of gods, to smaller figurines (for instance, for funerary use), to line drawings of gods and other beings (Ockinga 1984: 40–51; Schulz 1992: 707–8; Eschweiler 1994: 194–6). The word is derived from a root meaning 'to guide' or 'to lead', so that etymologically the word refers to the images as 'guides' or 'leaders'. Grammatically, an understanding of the word as a passive participle has been proposed (the Egyptian grammar and writing system allowing an interpretation as either active or passive in this case) based on the usage of the word to denote divine images carried out of the temple in festival processions, that is, images 'which are led' (Ockinga 1984: 40–1; cf. Eaton 2007: 18–19). However, for the majority of the images that the word can refer to, no such explanation would fit, and the earliest occurrences of the word refer to figurines and other images with no connection to processions. It thus seems most likely that the images themselves are thought of as 'guides' or 'leaders', a notion that will be discussed in more detail.

One way to interpret this etymology is to understand the image as a diagram or instruction meant to be followed (thus, e.g. Hoffmann 2001: 53, suggesting the meaning 'Vorbild'). While this understanding works for some uses of the designation, especially diagrams in two dimensions explicitly meant for copying, when used of images in three dimensions it becomes more problematic. Thus, one of the earliest uses of the term refers to a wooden image of the tomb owner, to be deposited in a chapel (cf. Nyord 2017), making it unlikely to have been intended as a model for further images.

A good example of how such images work comes from the so-called chapter 100 of the Book of the Dead (Lapp 1997: pls. 79–80, colour pl. II; Quirke 2013: 224–5; cf. Bryan 2017a: 10–11), a collection of ritual texts deposited in tombs. This particular text is meant for enabling its user to enter the barque of Re, in which the sun god was conceptualized as crossing the sky each day. This was accomplished by a recitation over an image showing the four deities Isis, Thoth, Khepri, and Shu as crew in the solar barque where they are joined by a smaller figure identified with the name of the owner of the papyrus (Fig. 4). In other words, the owner's presence in the solar barque was accomplished ritually by juxtaposing his *sšmw*-image with those of the solar barque and the gods present there.

How does the meaning of the image as a 'guide' relate to such a use of images? This can be elucidated by the so-called underworld book referred to in modern Egyptology as the 'Amduat' (Hornung 1963; Darnell and Darnell 2018: 127–248). The Amduat consists of a series of depictions and accompanying descriptions of the route travelled by the sun during its nightly absence from the sky, divided into twelve sections corresponding to the twelve hours of the night. The sun is shown vitalizing different cosmic processes, while the journey in turn simultaneously regenerates the sun god himself to allow him to rise invigorated in the east the next morning. The journey is said to take place in the Duat, an ancient Egyptian term for the 'under-' or 'otherworld', where transformative regeneration takes place out of sight of human beings (cf. Zago 2018). We know of the composition in the first instance because it was painted on the walls of royal tomb chambers during the Late Bronze Age from the fifteenth century BCE, while from the eleventh century BCE copies on papyrus were deposited in the tombs of non-royals.

The composition is of interest to us here because it repeatedly refers to the images of gods and other beings found in the Underworld as *sšmw*. Thus, in a characteristic passage, we read (Hornung 1963: II, 33):

> The images (*sšmw*) of the secret Powers are executed in this way, which is in writing in the hidden of the Duat, the beginning of the composition pointing westwards.

Fig. 4 Linen shroud of Tany with chapter 100 of the Book of the Dead.
The *sšmw*-images of (from right to left) the goddess Isis, and the gods Thoth,
Khepri, and Shu are joined by that of the owner of the linen (far left) in the solar
barque (only the prow and stern of which are preserved in this copy), effecting
her presence in their company. NMR.92 Nicholson Collection, Chau Chak
Wing Museum, The University of Sydney.

It is generally assumed that the composition of the Amduat is a representation of
a 'real' Underworld existing elsewhere, making the composition on tomb walls
into a kind of guidebook or map (e.g. Hornung 1999: 33). The implication of the
text's reference to *sšmw* would then be that this real Underworld is populated by

images of gods and other beings rather than by those beings themselves. As cogently argued over twenty years ago by Egyptologist Nadette Hoffmann, this leads to a potentially infinite regression where the images on tomb walls are images of the Underworld, which in turn holds images of something else, and so on. Hoffmann's suggested solution is to introduce a transcendent realm at one point or another where no further representations are possible (Hoffmann 1996: 38–40).

However, the references to images can also be understood non-representationally instead. In this case, the Amduat composition makes the burial chamber into an underworld, not by being modelled on the 'real' Underworld, but by enacting (or, to use the Egyptian word, 'guiding') the processes that need to take place for a space to be an underworld. That such a non-representational reading of the composition is preferable is indicated by the fact that later royal tombs draw eclectically on a number of different such compositions, whilst omitting significant parts of each of them (Hornung 1999: 27–31). If the images were a representation like a guidebook or map of the real Underworld, such 'remixing' would necessarily lead to false representations. If, on the other hand, the images instantiate particular regenerative processes that should take place in a tomb, such an eclectic approach becomes much easier to explain.

In this perspective, the images are most likely not meant primarily to resemble a 'real' Underworld existing somewhere else, but rather to effect the processes depicted, in turn making the space defined by the composition into an underworld in itself. The concept of *sšmw* can thus be understood similarly to the non-representational analysis of La Candelaria pots recently proposed by archaeologist Benjamin Alberti (2012: 24) where '[d]esign or image is not a representation of the source of transformation but the act of transformation itself'.

This understanding of the use of the concept in the Amduat has a number of implications for other images referred to by this term. If the images in the Amduat are thus thought to 'lead' that which they depict in the sense of enacting the configurations and processes depicted, this may also be true of other *sšmw*-images. This notion is immediately applicable to a case like the image accompanying chapter 100 of the Book of the Dead, which, as we have seen, aimed precisely to ritually establish the proximity between the human beneficiary and the gods that was depicted in the vignette itself.

Other *sšmw*-images can be understood as having a similar function. Thus, the class of funerary figurines known as *shabtis* (discussed in more detail in Section 4.3) was referred to using this term in the earliest textual references, and seems to have been employed at first precisely to effect the ritual presence of the depicted person in powerful places where he was not himself actually buried (Nyord 2017: 341–9). The notion that such images 'guide' or 'lead' the presence and configuration of what they depict thus seems to be a central characteristic shared by the different kinds of two- and three-dimensional images referred to by the term *sšmw*.

A corollary of this way of thinking about *sšmw*-images is that the actual viewing of, or interaction with, the images may be considered less important than is the case for other images, because their main purpose lay elsewhere, and in fact steps were often taken to make sure that such images were not seen. All of the examples of *sšmw*-images examined so far were either funerary or otherwise buried and taken out of circulation among humans. Even when such images were meant for use in the cult, it was often stressed how secret and secluded they were, to the point where the visibility of such images seems not only to be unnecessary for, but actually adverse to, their function of making that which they depict present. Thus, in a royal inscription, King Thutmose I (r. 1506–1493 BCE) describes his creation of the cult images for his monument in these terms: 'its *sšmw*-images were established for posterity, made efficacious and strictly secret, without being seen or gazed upon, without anyone knowing their shape' (*Urk.* IV, 97, 13–17). We will return to the importance of images being kept hidden in Section 3.4, but it is worth noting at this point how this aim is connected to *sšmw*-images in particular in a way that is clearly related to the conception of their function and use.

2.3 The Image as Bodily Presence: The Concept of *nfrw*

An important term, especially for divine images, is derived from the root *nfr*, usually translated as 'good' or 'beautiful'. In their generality, these translations do not give the material much chance to resist the interpretation – almost any positive quality can be rendered as either 'good' or 'beautiful' while retaining the overall sense of the passage in which they occur. However, there are indications that the meaning of the Egyptian root is at once more specific and more complex than these traditional renderings would suggest.

Apart from the relatively impoverished translations mentioned here, the root can sometimes be seen to have more specific meanings, most notably those of 'end, limit' in very concrete cases such as the innermost part of a tomb or dwelling, or a designation of the 'ground-level' in building construction (Frandsen 1992: 53–6). It can also have the meaning 'perfect(ed), complete(d), ripe' (Stock 1951; cf. Assmann 1969: 289) in certain connections. It is likely that the more general notions of 'good' and 'beautiful' should be understood as derivative of this central sense in contexts where these are the most salient properties of 'perfection'.

This somewhat elusive Egyptian concept bears comparison to Aristotle's notion of *entelecheia*, in the sense of full or completed actuality (e.g. Bechler 1995: 8–9). It is the 'end' for the sake of which each thing strives, so that, like the Egyptian concept of *nfr*, it can refer to completeness and perfection relative to a pertinent category. For things or beings belonging to categories where beauty or goodness are part of the ideal attributes, it can thus come to designate these things. Egyptologist Friedrich Junge has tentatively suggested a similar understanding when he proposed that *nfr* could be thought of as 'fulfillment (of the content of the concept)' ('Erfüllung des Begriffsinhaltes'; Junge 1990: 23 n. 55).

In light of this range of meanings, we can gloss the word as used with regard to the experience of deities as a 'material presence' with the additional nuance that this is thought of as being at the endpoint or apex of a scale on which a being can be more or less (perfectly) present. In turn, this 'presence' manifests itself in such observable phenomena as bodily or aesthetic beauty and perfection. It is further important to note that the experience of the presence of the god was not necessarily purely visual, as texts indicate that an epiphany could be accompanied by the smell of incense (Matić 2018: 44–7; Price 2018: 144–5), loud noises (Emerit 2011: 74–6; Manassa 2011: 152–66) or an embodied experience of 'awe' or 'terror' (Eicke 2017). A few examples will help to nuance the understanding of this at once both highly abstract and very concrete concept.

The ancient site of Abydos in Upper Egypt rose to unprecedented importance as a religious centre in the early second millennium BCE, and monuments from this site, along with references to its rituals in texts and images from elsewhere, provide the basis for much of our knowledge of cults to the gods in this period. A number of stelae (inscribed and decorated stone slabs) commemorate the participation of private people in the local rituals for the god Osiris, often having travelled far from their homes elsewhere in Egypt for this specific purpose. The characterization of the central participation in the ritual on a great many of these stelae describe it with combinations of stock phrases such as 'giving praise and kissing the ground for the great god and for Wepwawet, seeing his perfection (*nfrw*) at the First Procession, at the Great Procession, and at the god's journey to Peqer' (Cairo CG 20026, c 1–3; Lange and Schäfer 1902: 33). 'Giving praise' and 'kissing the ground' are standard ways of worshiping a god, while the notion of 'seeing the perfection' in turn focuses on the sensory (here primarily visual) experience of the presence of the god. This presence is often specifically ascribed to particular stages of the local festivities where the image of the god is carried in procession, thereby making it possible for the gathered people to gaze upon the material manifestation of the god.

During his reign in the mid-nineteenth century BCE, King Senwosret III sent his official Ikhernofret to Abydos in order to reinstate the rituals celebrated there. The first task in this process was the manufacturing of new cult images and other ritual equipment, and in his commemorative stela erected at Abydos, Ikhernofret gives the following description (Sethe 1928: 71, 2–6):

> I did everything which his Majesty had commanded in effectuating what my master had commanded for his father, Osiris Foremost-of-the-Westerners, Lord of Abydos, the Great Power in the Thinite District. I performed the role of the Loving Son for Osiris Foremost-of-the-Westerners, making effective for him the Great Bark for posterity and permanence. I made for him the bark shrine which displays the 'perfection' (*nfrw*) of the Foremost of the Westerners in gold, silver, lapis lazuli, copper, *sesnedjem*-wood, and cedar wood, and the gods in his suite were made.

As this passage makes clear, *nfrw* is used at once in the abstract sense of the material presence of the god within the shrine of the processional barque, while at the same time also referring concretely to the actual image displayed (or hidden, as the case may be) there. In fact, what makes usages like this understandable is that these two aspects are one and the same thing to the Egyptians, showing that the term *nfrw*, when used as an image designation, is a little more specialized than the other terms examined here in referring to the specific aspect of the divine image as the embodiment of a god, while notably avoiding the dualistic distinction we would intuitively make between an image as material object on the one hand and the presence of a god on the other.

While *nfrw* most centrally designated the divine image as the embodied, material presence of the god, this presence also spills over onto related objects. Thus, the ceremonial boat in which the statue of the god was carried can also be said to have *nfrw*, which no doubt in part plays on the nuance of the word to denote aesthetic qualities, but more centrally shows that the experience of divine presence radiates from the boat itself, even when the actual image is kept out of sight inside the cabin. Thus, towards the end of his inscription, Ikhernofret writes (Sethe 1928: 71, 18–20):

> I made him (sc. the god) proceed into the Great Bark, and it displayed his perfection (*nfrw*), as I made the eastern desert glad and created joy in the western desert when they saw the perfection (*nfrw*) of the *neshemet*-boat.

Here, *nfrw* is a trait both of the statue in the shrine as in the previous quotation, but also, by extension, of the boat itself, showing how the divine presence can spill over from the statue to objects or buildings holding it. Indeed, as shown by Ikhernofret's inscription, image and shrine would often be made of the same or a similar selection of materials, which may well have furthered this effect (see also Section 3.1). This type of emanation and scalability is typical of Egyptian experiences of divine presence.

A final example shows this phenomenon again, as well as illustrating that, although it usually is, the *nfrw*-embodiment of the god does not have to be an image in the strict sense. The notion that the ancient Egyptian king was a son of the sun god had a very long history. In the fifteenth century BCE, Hatshepsut had a particularly poignant expression of this idea (Fig. 5) inscribed on her mortuary temple on the western bank of Thebes (Deir el-Bahari), based on a version traceable in fragments back at least to the early second millennium BCE (cf. Quack 2018: 44 n. 30), and copied in turn by later kings. The inscription describes how the solar god Amun-Re desires a human woman (Hatshepsut's future mother) and descends to her, accompanied by the god Thoth, in order to sire a child (*Urk.* IV, 219, 12–220,6; cf. Brunner 1986: pl. 4):

> [Recitation by Amun-Re, Lord of the Thrones of the Two Lands, Foremost of his Ipet (Luxor), after he had made] his shape as the incarnation of this husband of hers, the Dual King Aakheperure. He found her sleeping in the innermost room of the palace. By the fragrance of the god she woke up, and she laughed before his incarnation. He went to her at once, having an erection toward her. He gave his heart to her and let her see him in his form of a god, after he had come close to her, as she rejoiced at the sight of his 'perfection' (*nfrw*). His love permeated her body, as the palace was inundated with the fragrance of a god, all his scents being those of Punt.

The 'shape' in which the god appears is not that of a statue in this case, but rather that of the living king. In political terms of royal succession, it is clear that this is meant to solve the problem of a new king in practice being (at least ideally) the son of his predecessor, while ideologically he was held to be sired by the sun god. Thus, we should most likely not understand this as a matter of 'disguise' in the sense of a ruse or deception allowing the queen to conceive a child with a person different from her husband. Rather, the notion of taking on a 'shape' here should be thought of as a matter of actually 'becoming', or perhaps we could gloss it as 'possessing', the body of the king. All the same, the god manifests an excess relative to the body of the king, so that his presence can be sensed in the first instance by the smell of incense thought to accompany the epiphany (as previously mentioned), and subsequently by revealing his full *nfrw*, which in this case is thus distinguished from the bodily form itself through a surplus of sensory stimulation.

The ideological figure of the Egyptian king raises a particular issue in this regard. Of divine origin and in some contexts understood himself to be a member of the category of *ntrw* ('gods'), the king nonetheless has a different status in terms of embodiment than other gods who are experienced primarily through their presence

Fig. 5 Formalized rendering of the encounter between the future mother of
Hatshepsut and the god Amun, which the accompanying text couches in
explicitly sexual terms. Line drawing by Henrijette Vex Nyord after Naville 1897: Pl.
47.

in statues, objects of power, and natural phenomena. This difference is captured
precisely by the concept of *nfr*, as a frequent designation of the king as opposed to
(most, cf. Tillier 2011) other gods is *nṯr nfr*, 'the young/perfect/present/fully
embodied god' (Stock 1951, Blumenthal 1970: 338; cf. Berlev 2003). While
most if not all gods can be ritually embodied in statues giving them *nfrw* in the
sense of material presence, this quality is thus nonetheless seen as particularly
characteristic of the king, whose embodiment is generally more advanced (in the
sense, perhaps, of being capable of a wider range of self-directed activities) and
stable. This parallelism between the images of a god and the body of the king is
particularly instructive for understanding the role of divine statues, and the two
categories could even overlap partially as seen in the case of the king's embodiment
of the god Amun-Re.

    As an image term, then, *nfrw* designates the statue as the 'perfection' or
'fullness' of the god's presence, a mode of existence which certainly implies

'beauty' as well, and more often than not costly and aesthetically pleasing materials and materiality.

2.4 The *ka* and the Image

Apart from the specific concepts that Egyptians used to refer to images, there is a long tradition in Egyptology of connecting one or another of the Egyptian 'soul' concepts to images, often explicitly to explain the problem of how such images came to be regarded as being alive. In the last two parts of this section, we will look at the evidence for regarding two central 'soul'-concepts as having this role in relation to images, namely the *ka* in this section, and the *ba* in the following.

Cult statues are often regarded in Egyptology as having a particularly close connection with the entity known in Egyptian as *ka* (*k3*). The *ka* is a difficult concept of central importance in ancient Egyptian mortuary religion, where most notably it is regarded as the recipient of offerings. Since offerings were generally presented in front of an image (in two or three dimensions), this would seem to offer a firm point of connection between image and *ka*. However, remarkably few ancient Egyptian texts make any connection between these two entities, and when they do, only quite indirectly (Fitzenreiter 2001: 545–8; Nyord 2019: 156). This means that, as entrenched as it is in Egyptological tradition, the idea that the cult statue is the dwelling place of, or even identical to, the *ka* is purely conjectural.

This state of affairs has meant that most Egyptologists have more or less deliberately perpetuated the idea of the statue as home of the *ka*, while a smaller group have rejected the idea categorically from lack of evidence, without much prospect of either resolving the disagreement or reconciling the positions. However, a reinterpretation of the *ka* concept may hold the potential for explaining how the *ka* and the image came to be so closely associated in cultic practice, while at the same time being kept conceptually distinct.

According to this interpretation, the *ka* is not so much a soul-like aspect of the person, but is rather the potential of which a human being is the manifestation in a broad sense spanning what we would categorize as hereditary, behavioural, and spiritual properties (Nyord 2019). Thus, the *ka* is the originator both of the existence of the human being as a kind of life force, and of the behaviour and predilections of a person as a deeper-rooted 'personality' or 'self'. The bridge between these apparently quite different roles of the *ka* can be found in the prevalent ancient Egyptian notion of cyclical creation: even something that appears relatively fixed, such as a human individual, is in fact the result of an ongoing process of becoming. Thus, the *ka* is involved in a similar way in decisive events such as the conception and birth of a new human being, and in continuing processes of behavior and development. According to this idea, a person's body and the affects it holds would be another direct effect of the *ka*. As has been seen in the previous sections, there are a number of considerations determining the suitability of a particular statue as an image of a specific individual, and, if the interpretation of the *ka* sketched here is correct, it would stand to reason that these fundamental questions of compatibility would have been regarded as being dependent on the *ka* – like any other affects of the person.

2.5 The *ba* and the Image

The *ba* is the second main candidate for a notion akin to a 'soul', often depicted in the shape of a human-headed stork (Fig. 6). Briefly put, the *ba* constitutes the capacity of a being to become manifest, and while living human beings do seem to have one, they play a role mainly for less fixed and spatially bound entities such as ancestors or gods. As such, one could easily expect an idea where the 'life' found in the statue is present there by virtue of the *ba*. However, clear, direct evidence for such an idea is found only very late in Egyptian history, at a time when Egyptian religion was under the influence of Greek and Roman thought (Assmann 2001 [1984]: 40–4; Assmann 2009: 83–7; cf. Eschweiler 1994: 289).

A single, much-earlier, but somewhat uncertain, passage has been taken to indicate the significant antiquity of such ideas. The passage comes from a prayer inscribed on a series of stelae during the fifteenth century BCE. In a translation following the text as it stands, the passage reads (*Urk.* IV, 1526, 8–1527, 5):

> May I walk on the bank of my pool without cease,
> may my *ba* alight on the branches (*ꜥḥm*) of the garden (*mnw*) that I made,
> may I cool off under my sycamore trees.

At first sight, it seems clear that this passage refers to the ability of the deceased to return to the tomb, in particular to take pleasure in the garden planted outside of the tomb. However, in an influential exposition of ancient Egyptian conceptions of the divine, Jan Assmann has suggested a different reading based on the fact that the word *ꜥḥm* can mean not only branches, but also a divine image or some kind of nature spirit, while *mnw* has the related meanings of not just 'garden', but also 'monument' (Assmann 2001 [1984]: 43). In the hieroglyphic writing system, however, these words are generally distinguished, and the writings of the words in the passage indicate the meaning as 'branches' and 'garden' as rendered in the quoted translation. This thus points in the same direction as the overall context, where both the preceding

Fig. 6 Wooden statuette of the *ba* in its characteristic form of a human-headed
bird. Michael C. Carlos Museum, 1999.1.139. © Michael C. Carlos Museum,
Emory University. Photo by Peter Harholdt.

and following lines deal with the topic of the *ba* visiting a garden, making
a reference to images in the tomb unexpected. Moreover, closer examination of
the usage of the word ꜥḥm as reference to images (Hoffmann 2001: 139, 519;
Eaton 2007: 17) has shown that it is used of divine images in animal form, but
not usually for anthropomorphic images, nor (for that reason) in the context of
the tomb. If a reference to images were intended here, it is thus unlikely that this
word would have been chosen among the many possibilities (a few of which
were examined in the preceding sections).

There are a few other, roughly contemporary, passages that are sometimes
mentioned in the same breath as this one, although they generally offer evidence
that is much less clear and could only be used to support the idea of the *ba*
descending upon images once this notion had been firmly established. Thus, for
example, a limestone statue of one Panehesy from the thirteenth century BCE

has an inscription addressed directly to the statue, reading: 'May incense and natron be given to you by those left behind by your master. Then the *ba* will come hurrying to receive offering bread together with you' (*KRI* III, 137, 10; cited in this connection by Assmann 2009: 89; cf. most recently Frood 2019: 11–12). Unless one has already concluded that the *ba* comes to reside inside the statue as the real recipient of the offerings, however, the text does not have to be understood this way. Strictly speaking, it only tells us that the *ba* can come to receive offerings, and in fact the wording of the *ba* and the statue both receiving the offerings together (and thus on a par) might be taken to indicate a different, less hierarchical understanding.

At any rate, Assmann's discussion cites a number of examples from the Late and Graeco-Roman Periods a millennium or so later, where there is in fact a clear idea of the *ba*s of gods entering their images in the temple (Assmann 2001 [1984]: 40–4). The question thus becomes whether this is an idea that is characteristic only of the later periods, or whether it can be taken as relevant throughout Egyptian history. Assmann's interpretation of the quoted stela passage implies the latter interpretation, and this understanding has been very popular since Assmann first introduced it in 1984, to the point where it is often quoted as a standard explanation for why the Egyptians made statues (e.g. Hartwig 2004: 38; Meskell 2004: 91–2, 102; Kjølby 2009: 38; cf. also Nyord 2017: 340 n. 4; more indirectly in Braun 2009: 109).

I have already referred to the philological problems questioning the reading of the passage as a reference to images, but there are further chronological problems as well. Even if accepted, the reference to the *ba* alighting on the statue would be the earliest attestation of this notion, occurring at a time when tomb statues and decorated tomb chapels had been prevalent in elite burials for more than 1,000 years. Moreover, textual references to the *ba* throughout this period evidence a gradual development of the concept (Žabkar 1968), which means that we can more or less rule out this idea as an original motivation for Egyptian statue practices: the concept of the *ba* simply does not seem to have had the required characteristics at the time when statues were first made (cf. Eschweiler 1994: 290). The idea of the inert image enlivened by the descending soul is most clearly expressed in the Graeco-Roman Period, and indeed it smacks of a dualism between spirit and matter that is difficult to attest in Egyptian thought of earlier periods. In fact, it was first applied to the earlier period especially by Egyptologist and historian of religion Siegfried Morenz in his efforts to explain how the concept of a transcendent god could arise in Egypt (Morenz 1964: 34–6). Together, these facts make Assmann's understanding of the fifteenth-century inscription as simply an early expression of the same idea even more problematic.

2.6 Conclusion: Egyptian Image Concepts

The discussion of the two Egyptian 'soul' concepts, *ka* and *ba*, showed that the evidence connecting these notions to images was rare and vague for the vast majority of ancient Egyptian history. These problems run somewhat deeper than merely being a question of whether we can project very late evidence back in time and assume that it was relevant in earlier periods as well. Rather, they raise the question of whether the idea of a dogmatic belief in a 'ghost in the machine' (whether that role is assigned to the *ka* or the *ba*) is really an accurate reflection of Egyptian thought. As will be seen in Section 3, the notion of 'inert' matter fails to do justice to Egyptian experiences, so that there may quite simply have been no need for a quickening 'spirit' in the sense we might expect.

The vagueness and range of conceptualizations found in the sources suggest that Egyptian uses of images were less a one-to-one deployment of dogmatic beliefs, and that we are more likely to be dealing with conceptions developed and maintained through ritual practice and imagistic intuition. When pressed to make a theoretical explanation of such concepts ultimately based on concrete experience, it is typical that members of the society may well come up with quite different interpretations (see e.g. Boyer 1994). Such a process of theoretical explication of traditional beliefs was particularly prevalent in the Late and Graeco-Roman Periods where almost all of the evidence for the *ba* entering statues comes from (e.g. Assmann 1992).

This means that we are better off seeking an approach suited to uncover such more general perceptions of the role of images, and in particular their relationship to that which they depict. The image terminology discussed in this section is valuable in this regard, but before we examine its implications, there is another traditional idea that needs to be discussed. Egyptian conceptions of images are sometimes described along the lines that the Egyptians did (or even could) not distinguish between a depiction and that which it depicts (especially frequently in the traditional idea that images of offerings in tombs could be enjoyed by the deceased in the same way as actual offerings, e.g. Kanawati 2001: 115–21). In a sense, this is the logical polar opposite to the notion of representationalism criticized earlier, but it is also a problematic claim. Such an idea is not limited to Egyptology, but was a deeply entrenched allegation concerning traditional societies in the twentieth century (see e.g. the brief discussion in Eschweiler 1994: 291–3, and cf. e.g. Neer 2017 for the discussion in ancient Greek art). It is, however, clearly unreasonable, as demonstrable by a wide range of cultural practices as well as in language where for the most part the Egyptians make clear distinctions between 'X' and 'an image of X'.

However, the examination of some central Egyptian image terms allows us to make a somewhat more nuanced characterization of Egyptian images than either of the two extremes of representationalism at one end of the spectrum and the equation between depiction and depicted at the other. At the same time, the rejection of the traditional explanations along the lines of one or the other Egyptian 'soul' living in the statue means that we can approach the question in a more targeted way. So what *does* Egyptian image terminology tell us about the relationship between a depiction and what it depicts, if it is neither a question of a complete identity nor of a 'soul' dwelling in the image?

The discussion of the term *twt* showed that while Egyptian art is in one sense characterized by the aim of achieving 'likeness', the Egyptian notion of what it means for an image to resemble what it depicts is somewhat different from what we might intuitively expect. Rather than attempting to capture incidental details of the visual appearance of an individual, images aim to present adequately the deeper, underlying nature of the depicted entity. This results in the characteristic tendency for Egyptian depictions to idealize, and also helps account for the fact that many Egyptian images depict human beings in a way so that iconography, posture, and other details essentially serve to categorize the depicted entity. Thus, we see the tomb owner depicted, for example, 'as a scribe' sitting cross-legged with a scroll in his lap, or in the standard seated or standing pose as a dignitary ready to receive petitioners (cf. the example in two dimensions in Fig. 16). To kings, different statue types were available, such as the human-headed sphinx or other forms entailing a close association with the divine. An image blending these categories, such as a statue of a private person with physiognomy of the reigning king (or even a great king of the past) is an embodiment that both demonstrates and elicits the shared nature of the persons 'blended' visually and conceptually in this way. Our examination of the *twt* concept thus reveals the underlying sense in which the image, while not a mimetic representation in our sense, needed to be adequate and appropriate to the kind of being depicted.

The term *sšmw* highlights a different aspect of Egyptian image concepts, namely the idea of the image as a 'guide' or 'leader' effecting the presence and/or configuration of entities depicted. In some cases, this led to situations where the depiction was explicitly not, as we would tend to assume from a representationalist point of view, a depiction of an already-existing reality or situation, but rather a way to effect ritually the relationship depicted. The question of space becomes particularly important in this use of images, as the aim will often be to effect the presence of the depicted entity where the depiction is deposited, or even, as in the case of the Amduat, to transform an entire space to enable the relationships and processes depicted to take place there.

Finally, the notion of *nfrw* showed that images could have a significant overlap with bodies, especially as the central part of the sensory impression caused by the presence of a god. In particular, the term effortlessly straddled two senses that we would tend to see as clearly separate, namely the image of the god as a 'physical' object on the one hand, and the presence of the god as a 'subjective' religious experience on the other. Another noteworthy feature is that the *nfrw* did not have to be figurative representation, but could also be a feature of non-representational objects such as a processional barque for transporting the god's image, or even the body of the reigning king.

In sum, the Egyptian terminology examined here troubles representationalist expectations in a number of ways regarding the relationship between the depiction and that which it depicts. A mimetic representation can be either good or bad, even true or false, depending on the degree of likeness to the depicted entity. An Egyptian image cannot be judged in this way, since it does not stand in a representationalist relationship to what it depicts. At best, it can be more or less suited as an embodiment of a given entity depending on its adequacy to that entity's 'nature' or classificatory category. Similarly, a map-like depiction of the Underworld could be good or bad depending on its accuracy vis-à-vis reality, whereas a *sšmw*-image of underworld processes becomes more a matter of the appropriateness of what is depicted to the space in which the images are placed and the rituals with which they are activated. For this reason, Egyptian discourses about images are rarely occupied with whether an image is right or wrong, but instead with what the image can do where it is deployed.

It is useful at this point to compare the emerging pattern with Assyriologist Zainab Bahrani's study of the Mesopotamian concept of *ṣalmu* (Bahrani 2003: 121–48). Bahrani argues that Assyro-Babylonian images can be understood as one of a number of interrelated ways of encountering the person, including also the name, the 'organic body', offspring, a body double, and more. Rather than standing in any particular hierarchy (such as the image being a mere copy subordinated to the organic body), these elements instead constitute 'a pluridimensional chain of possible appearances' (Bahrani 2003: 128). In her conclusion on the concept of *ṣalmu*, Bahrani sets up the following set of oppositions, which recalls several of the conclusions concerning Egyptian image terminology (Bahrani 2003: 137):

> Ṣalmu is not an objective representation of reality. It is not a represented truth about the person, nor is it a representational lie about the person, as in propaganda. Ṣalmu, as a mimetic representation, may relate to the object as an excess in that it can act as a repetition, a replacement. But it is not an element that represents the whole.

The idea of the image as one among a range of possible ways of encountering an entity is useful in thinking about Egyptian images as well. Like the Mesopotamian king studied by Bahrani, Egyptians also considered the human being to incorporate numerous aspects, several of which, such as the body or the *ba*, could explicitly on occasion function as a way of encountering the entire entity. As we have seen, this is also true of images. The relationship between depiction and depicted in ancient Egypt, then, is one where the image serves as a material presence of the person depicted, not (necessarily) by being inhabited by a soul, or being a mimetic copy of a body, but simply by virtue of the inherent connection established in a variety of partly overlapping ways (apart from being understood as adequate to the kind of being depicted) such as being inscribed with a name, being ritually dedicated, being deposited in a particular place, or simply by being understood to stand in such a relationship by its maker(s) and/or user(s).

This preliminary examination has already brought us a significant step closer to understanding Egyptian imaging practices. However, in an important sense, examining images only from the perspective of a bilateral relationship between depiction and depicted is highly reductive, however central this aspect is. Thus, as shown in Alfred Gell's influential classic *Art and Agency* (Gell 1998), this relationship is only one of many 'indexed' by a work of art in a network including artists, patrons, audiences, etc. (cf. Kjølby 2009 for an Egyptological application). For most places and times in pharaonic Egypt, we have very little knowledge about the broader social networks and institutions surrounding the production and use of images, as we are usually dependent on the knowledge that can be gleaned from the artwork itself along with its place and manner of deposition (when these have been recorded by excavators). With this limitation in mind, however, the evidence we do have of the material, social, and discursive networks of which images were part will be the topic for the next section.

3 Making and Encountering Images

The discussion in Section 2 has given a sense of central aspects of Egyptian understandings of images, especially regarding the relationship between depiction and depicted. In this section, we will examine the ways in which images formed part of much larger networks of people and things.

The materials of which images were made naturally played a crucial role. As has already been indicated by the preceding discussion of image concepts, the Egyptians did not share our intuition of materials as inert substances waiting to be given shape and meaning by a human hand. Rather materials themselves held particular kinds of power, making each material potentially more or less suitable for a given task, and lending particular forms of agency to the image. The first part of this section examines such perceptions of materials.

In ancient Egypt, image-makers or 'artists' remained for the most part anonymous. When images are inscribed with names, it is predominantly those of the patron depicted or other persons in his or her social group, but almost never the maker. This means that the images themselves provide only indirect evidence of the identity of the maker(s) and the processes that led to their creation. However, a number of other sources do provide occasional insights into the interplay between artists, patrons, and the wider social networks of which they were part.

Another side of the social life of images is that of their reception by intended or unintended audiences. A chief question in this regard is that of aesthetics. A defining feature of some cross-cultural definitions of 'art' (e.g. Baines 2015: 2–3), aesthetic concerns nonetheless do not square straightforwardly with the kind of relational functions of the image that were examined in the last section. This raises the question of how aesthetics and function relate to each other. Presumably the Egyptians would have been able to judge an image as 'beautiful' or 'ugly', but would that also make it a 'good' or 'bad' image? Section 3.3 takes up such questions.

Section 3.4 explores the phenomenon of images fulfilling their function without being seen, or only being seen under very restricted circumstances and/or by highly limited audiences. This shows that images go well beyond strictly visual concerns, which leads to further considerations regarding their mode of function.

These discussions lead to a central concept in the understanding of images espoused here, namely that of 'affect' (in the sense of capacity to affect or be affected), under which heading features of an image such as iconography can be considered in a new key (Section 3.5). If the function of images is first and foremost as relation-makers, then the ways such relations are elicited materially become a pivotal question for their role in networks of people, places, and powers.

3.1 Materials That Matter

There is ample evidence that ancient Egyptian image-makers made very deliberate choices about the materials from which images were made. In fact, it is likely that this intuitive way of phrasing the use of materials may turn the question on its head as seen from the Egyptian point of view: Materials held a primacy and power that we fail to capture if we think of artistic creation merely as a matter of applying a preconceived form to an inert material. The example of the experiences related by a quarrying expedition illustrates this point.

The Wadi Hammamat is a valley through the desert east of the Nile, leading from the ancient city of Koptos north of modern-day Luxor to the Red Sea coast.

Cutting through the desert mountains, the valley exposes layers of a number of different stones valued by the Egyptians, making it a desirable, if somewhat inhospitable, destination for quarrying expeditions (cf. Aufrère 1991: 79–81). Among the inscriptions commemorating these activities, a group from an expedition organized by the Vizier Amenemhat for King Mentuhotep IV (r. 1998–1991 BCE) to quarry a block for a sarcophagus lid stand out (Strandberg 2009: 170–3). In two of the inscriptions left behind by the expedition, it is recorded how two different 'wonders' mark a specific block as special through divine revelation. The first shows how this particular block was singled out by providence as particularly appropriate for the purpose of a sarcophagus lid (Couyat and Montet 1912: 77–8 and pl. 29):

> The wonder which happened for his Incarnation: The desert animals came down to him. A pregnant gazelle came walking, her eyes looking straight ahead. She did not turn around until she reached this noble mountain and this block, while it was still in its place, for the lid of the sarcophagus. She gave birth on it, while this expedition force of the king watched. Then her throat was cut, and she was placed on it (sc. the sarcophagus lid) as a burnt offering.

The use of the word *bꜣ*, 'wonder' or 'epiphany', as well as the fact that the episode was deemed important enough to record, shows that the arrival of the gazelle was regarded as no mere coincidence, but that it was seen as revealing something fundamental about the nature of the block. The religious associations of the gazelle and the behavior related here are wide-ranging (see the brief discussion in Strandberg 2009: 170–3), but of particular relevance are the role of the gazelle as an embodiment of the desert environment, making her first kin to the stones of the cliffs, and the ritual notion that the lid of a coffin or sarcophagus embodies the sky-goddess Nut thought to swallow the sun god each night and give birth to him each morning. Thus, the gazelle simultaneously singles out the block from amongst other possible choices at the quarry and reveals its particular fit for the purpose of the sarcophagus lid.

Another inscription records a second wonder which happened twenty days later, once again affirming the special nature of the block at a point when work on extracting the block was well underway. A flash flood placed the lower part of the quarry under water, with the surface of the water reaching the block being quarried, turning it into an island in a sudden lake (which also revealed a well for fresh water, the availability of which was a prime concern on mining and quarrying expeditions).

As unusual as they are, these wondrous occurrences are instructive for the underlying perception of materials. Far from being inert raw materials, they are 'vibrant' substances (in the words of Bennett 2010) entangled with, and always carrying with them, the places from which they came, and the powers captured through (and indicated by) their materiality and biography. In this way, the wondrous events related in the inscriptions are relevant because they reveal hitherto-hidden aspects of the stone block, laying bare parts of its relationships to landscape, cosmic processes, and divine powers. They are recorded, in turn, because they illustrate the extraordinary (and hence prestigious) nature of the sarcophagus lid, along with the special status of the king to whom it was revealed.

While the inscriptions focus on miraculous events, in many cases a significant part of the powers inherent in the materials are no doubt reflected (and revealed) by their sensory qualities, or materiality (e.g. Raven 1988; Wilkinson 1994: 82–125; Baines 2007: 263–80; Sist 2016). Thus, for example, quartzite (silicified sandstone) boasts a reddish-orange colour and yields a brilliantly reflective surface when polished smooth (Fig. 7). Perhaps aided by its principal site of quarrying near Heliopolis, the sacred city of the sun god, these qualities give quartzite a strong solar association (e.g. Connor 2016–2017: 15–16). However, we would most likely be amiss if we think of this connection primarily as a matter of 'symbolism' in the sense of a conventional reference allowing the sender to communicate an idea to the receiver. To the Egyptian, the qualities of the stone would rather be perceived as revealing an intrinsic connection or consubstantiality with the sun, whether in a given case this was primarily experienced as the stone sharing a quality of 'sun-ness' and/or vice versa.

Similarly, when a number of written sources attest to the notion that gods have flesh of gold, this should also be taken more literally than we might be inclined to. The use of gold (or its imitations) in an object like a coffin is not primarily meant to communicate to an audience the abstract idea of the divinity of the deceased; rather it transforms the materiality of the body of the deceased to make him or her consubstantial with the bodies of the gods – thereby effecting, rather than expressing, divinity. By extension, we can conjecture that this must have been the case with all materials from which divine images were made, even when we have no written sources confirming it for a particular material: If the material was fit to be the embodiment of a god, it must have held the potential for a connection with that god. As Jan Assmann has put it: 'In a certain sense, divinity already dwells in the stone and is accorded a shape by the stonecutter, which can then become the vessel for a specific cultic habitation ["*Einwohnung*"]' (Assmann 2009: 94). The sentiment is similar to the approach to materials presented here, though the dualistic notions of a 'vessel' and 'habitation' are perhaps best avoided as discussed previously.

If divine powers thus inhere in the materials from the outset, how can we understand the act of shaping materials into an image? The so-called

Fig. 7 Quartzite head of Amenhotep III embodying qualities of solar rejuvenation. Metropolitan Museum of Art, 56.138.

hylomorphic idea (Simondon 1964; cf. Ingold 2013: 17–31), where an abstract shape is applied to an inert material, clearly is not very helpful. According to the 'analogist' mode of thinking (cf. Section 1), the same interpretive principle of understanding symbolic connections as revealing ontological ones is helpful in thinking about shape as well. Shaping an object according to conventional iconography, then, is also not primarily an act of communication (though it may certainly serve that purpose as well), but rather the capturing in a material form of the powers that the 'icon' expresses. Further, as such shapes in a certain sense exist as potentials in the material before it is moulded, cut, or carved, we can also think of image motifs as an act of drawing out these potentials from the potentialities inhering in the material. We will return to some consequences of this way of understanding materials in Section 3.4.

Synthetic materials offer particular affordances in this regard (cf. Gibson 1966 for the concept). Egyptian faience is a non-clay ceramic technology made from materials that would have been readily available to many Egyptian town or village dwellers (Miniaci 2018). The primary method of producing the shiny (usually blue or bluish-green) glazing is that of efflorescence, where the colouring agents are mixed into the ceramic paste to emerge to the surface as the paste dries, and then melt and fuse to the object when fired (Fig. 8). This process of manufacture would have provided a salient instantiation of the widespread Egyptian principle of creation by emergence, according to which the differences of the created world emanate from an originary unity. This is not only an abstract theological idea expressed in myth, but finds experiential correlates in the flooding and subsequent receding of the Nile as well as a number of other natural phenomena. Some of the most striking uses of Egyptian faience (cf. Nyord 2020) draw out precisely this conceptual affordance through painted patterns of such motifs as hippopotamuses (amphibious creatures able to emerge from the waters and disappear again without warning), water lilies (emerging from the waters and opening and closing in concert with the solar cycle) and *tilapia* fish (mouth-brooders apparently emitting small fractal copies of itself from the mouth only to let them reenter if threats are perceived).

This role of materials as powerful in their own right, rather than an inert substrate waiting to be given significant shape, can be illustrated further by the so-called *jeux de la nature* (Keimer 1940). These are objects found naturally with a recognizable shape, which was then brought out by the addition of a few strokes of a brush – in turn helping the modern observer recognize what the Egyptian saw in the object. In a number of cases from the village of Deir el-Medina (discussed in more detail in Section 3.2), such objects share a range of motifs with more deliberately created images, indicating that they may have been used similarly (Weiss 2015: 153–4). These minimal images were often made of the flint available in abundance in the cliffs around the village, and there is ample evidence that this material was experienced as powerful in its own right (Desroches-Noblecourt 2003: 56–9; Graves-Brown 2006; Graves-Brown 2010). The mountains west of Thebes where Deir el-Medina is located were perceived as the embodiment of the goddess Hathor (Rummel 2016), and flint nodules shaped like women that have seemingly detached themselves from the cliffs whose substance they share will have been experienced as particularly concentrated crystallizations of the power of fertility and regeneration instantiated by that deity.

Not surprisingly, Egyptian image-makers developed great expertise in not only enabling, but also playing with, these material manifestations of power. This can lead to cases where the communicative use of iconography seems clearly to overshadow the 'vibrant' role of the material. A notable example is a statue of Queen Mutemwiya (early fourteenth century BCE) made of the hard, black stone known as granodiorite and set up in the Karnak Temple by her son Amenhotep III as focus for the cult of the queen (Kozloff, Bryan, and Berman 1992: 126; cf. Müller 2003: 87; Fig. 9). The queen is depicted seated on a throne in turn located inside a boat of the type used in religious processions for transporting the divine image. The figure of the queen herself is embraced from behind by the wings of

Fig. 8 Faience cup in the form of a lotus flower, with form and material both materializing aquatic powers of emergence and creation. Metropolitan Museum of Art, 26.7.972.

a large vulture, an embodiment of the goddess Mut, one of the chief deities of the Karnak Temple complex.

This particular combination of iconography is highly unusual, and there is no doubt that it has been chosen in order to establish a rebus for the queen's name, as Mutemwia literally means '(the goddess) Mut (is) in the processional boat'. In this way, the image of the queen becomes entangled with that of the goddess, both as the embracing figures in the boat, and because the entire statue becomes an expression of the queen's name. This makes the statue closely akin to written communication. However, it also works along the non-communicative lines explored here, since the sculpture functions at the same time as an embodiment of the queen presented and protected by, as well as identified with, the vulture goddess. Thus, simultaneously with working on the level of the rebus tying it to a specific queen, and on the level of a more general ideological statement, the statue is also a capturing of powers of the goddess in her processional manifestation in an embodiment of queen-and-goddess capable of effecting their material presence in the cult.

3.2 Artists, Patrons, and Commissioners

As mentioned, the identities of image-makers and their relationships to patrons and commissioners tend to be masked by the traditional ancient Egyptian

Fig. 9 Granodiorite statue of Queen Mutemwia embodying the goddess Mut in her processional boat, while at the same time displaying a 'rebus' of the queen's name. British Museum, EA 43. © Trustees of the British Museum.

discourses about images (e.g. Quirke 2003; Laboury 2013). This is clearly consonant with the functional view of an image as a way to establish a relationship to the depicted entity, so that the technical skill with which it was carried out was primarily a means to an end, or when explicitly recognized, added to the renown of the patron rather than that of the artist. While thus fitting better with modern notions of 'craft' than of 'art', such a relatively withdrawn role of image-makers – often, as in Egypt, accompanied by a lack of distinction corresponding to our 'craft' versus 'art' – is by no means unusual in traditional societies (see e.g. several of the contributions in d'Azevedo 1989 [1973]).

Partly for this reason, makers of images have tended to be somewhat overlooked in Egyptological exploration of Egyptian art, and one often looks in vain for them in overviews and handbooks (cf. Riggs 2017: 299). Similarly, though 'workshops' are frequently discussed, the term tends to be used mostly as a convenient shorthand for clusters of typological features, possibly associated with a particular locality, rather than as units of social organization of interest in their own right (e.g. Eschenbrenner-Diemer 2017; Ilin-Tomich 2017), although such studies can certainly reveal social connections, for instance, between the private and royal sphere (e.g. Hartwig 2004: 30–5). In recent years, however, a resurgence of interest in these largely hidden persons has resulted in several publications devoted to ancient Egyptian artists and their activities (e.g. Angenot and Tiradritti 2016; Gillen 2017; Miniaci et al. 2018).

An exceptional, and correspondingly frequently discussed, inscription of an artist who presents his artistic expertise in some detail has survived from around 2000 BCE (Louvre C 14). The owner of the stela, Irtysen, presents himself as an 'overseer of craftsmen, scribe, and sculptor' – note that 'craftsmen' here could equally be translated as 'artists', as the Egyptian language does not make a distinction between what we would call 'craft' and 'art'. Instead of the traditional self-laudatory praises of the owner as an ethical and loyal official, Irtysen's inscription presents his knowledge of the secrets of the image-maker in a dense text with numerous unique and uniquely used words that have made its precise translation a subject of ongoing debate (see most recently Mathieu 2016; Bryan 2017b; Stauder 2018; Fitzenreiter 2019). Andréas Stauder has cogently noted that the text would most likely have caused similar problems even to literate readers of its time, adding a further layer to Irtysen's repeated stress of his mastery of secret knowledge and expertise (Stauder 2018: 262). A rendering of Irtysen's self-presentation might read:

(Ritual knowledge)
I know the restricted knowledge of hieroglyphs and the conduct of festivals. All *ḥkꜣ*-power, I have equipped myself with it, with nothing thereof escaping me. As such, I am a craftsman skilled in his craft, one who has come out on top because of what he has learned.

(Knowledge of grids and proportions)
I know the parts of the inert one(?), the upholding of correct proportions, how to subtract and add as it goes out or in, so that (each) body part ends up in its right place.

(Knowledge of posture and scene composition)
I know the stride of a (male) figure, the steps of a female figure, the stance of numerous birds, the incline of one smiting a sole (captive), one eye looking at its fellows, how to make fearful the face of the (bound) enemy, the lifting of the arm of one spearing a hippopotamus, and the steps of one who runs.

(Knowledge of enduring techniques)
I know how to make pigments and the things that go into them, without letting fire burn them, nor can they be washed away with water.

(The transmission of knowledge)
No-one reveals it to anyone, except me alone and my eldest bodily son, for the god has decreed that he perform the duty of the one to whom it is revealed. I have seen his proficiency in acting as overseer of works in every precious material from silver and gold to ebony and ivory.

The overall outline of the image-maker which emerges from this description is characteristic and generally confirmed by other insight we have into their self-perception and social standing. As in other traditions, the stress of knowledge is paramount, as one would expect from the generally rule-bound and conventional nature of Egyptian art. As has already been implied in the examination of image terminology in the previous section, the knowledge of such conventions and techniques intermingles with knowledge of a more ritual nature. In fact, his ritual knowledge is the first thing Irtysen stresses, and it is even possible to understand several of the subsequent expressions also as references to ritual concerns (as argued by Bryan 2017b). It is worth noting that while this very close entanglement of a high level of ritual expertise with more technical aspects of image-making may not be entirely typical, there is ample evidence of craftsmen playing a central role in rituals, going well beyond the kind of tangibly technical tasks we might expect (Chauvet 2015).

An interesting detail concerning the social role of the image-maker is that on the one hand he stresses his unique knowledge (much of which must, however, have been shared or replicated by other master craftsmen), yet on the other hand he has the title of 'overseer of craftsmen', so that we should imagine him as being, in practice, the head of one or more workshops (cf. also Quirke 2003). The craftsmen in such workshops must have been privy to some of the practical knowledge described, so the master's distinction seems to come from his broad command of techniques and conventions (cf. Laboury 2017), and perhaps especially with the coupling of this with his knowledge of rites and ritual efficacy. Finally, this knowledge is not passed on to the most skilled or senior of the journeymen, but more specifically, it is hereditary and is passed on to Irtysen's eldest son – albeit only because it is mandated by the god, and in the recognition that he has proven himself a worthy successor (see von Lieven 2007 for the initiation of artists).

A very different, and several centuries later, window into the lives of image-makers comes from the already-mentioned village with the modern name of Deir el-Medina (see e.g. McDowell 2002; Meskell 2002). The village was a planned settlement meant to house the craftsmen working on the rock-cut royal tombs in the Valley of the Kings during the mid-to-late second millennium BCE. Located in the mountains some way from the Nile, this was a secluded community with careful monitoring of access and flow of goods. Populated by royally commissioned artisans and their families, the village exhibits an unusually high level of literacy as well as extraordinary concern among the inhabitants with artistic creation. Like other Egyptians of their class, the inhabitants of the village needed images for a number of different purposes in life and death, and because of their secluded existence, combined with the special skills of many inhabitants, it was natural for them to produce such images themselves. At the same time, their narrowly circumscribed lives and high level of literacy meant that the inhabitants often ended up carrying out transactions concerning images in writing, much of which is still extant in the so-called *ostraca*, pottery sherds or flakes of the local limestone which provided handy and portable surfaces for writing and drawing.

One such ostracon (Moje 2006) from the thirteenth or twelfth century BCE is a note telling a craftsman not mentioned by name to produce an image: 'Please have brought to me in all haste today, take good care: An image (*twt*) of Montu seated on a throne with an image (*twt*) of the scribe Pentawere kissing the ground before him, worshiping him, in line drawing' (K*RI* V, 566, 7–9).

The instruction specifies the technique (line drawing), while the medium remains implicit. However, the fact that the image is to be brought to the writer shows that the message must concern an image in a portable medium, a stela or perhaps most likely another ostracon. This means that the image may have been intended as a sketch for a larger-scale painting, though ostraca could also, like stelae, function as cultic focal points in their own right (Weiss 2015: 158–61). The amount of knowledge taken for granted shows that members of the community assumed each other to be familiar enough with divine iconography and conventions of layout and inscription to produce the requested drawing from the terse instructions. Many such portable drawings of religious scenes of one or more persons worshiping a particular god have been found at Deir el-Medina (Weiss 2015: 383–426; Fig. 10), though none that matches this instruction exactly, perhaps because expressions like 'kissing the ground' should be understood more generally to indicate a different act of worship (Walsem 1982: 194).

Other sources from the west bank of Thebes provide evidence for a number of other aspects of the social setting of the artists working in the necropoleis there (Hartwig 2004: 22–35). For private tomb chapels, it seems that access to the required skilled labour depended on the more-or-less formal networks of the patron, because craftsmen tended to be part of state or institutional workshops. However the labour was procured, there is good evidence that a well-stocked decorated tomb must have been a costly affair (Hartwig 2004: 26–7; Cooney 2007).

Perhaps not surprisingly, documents from Deir el-Medina also show religious images as forming a central part of social and economical transactions in the community. Thus several documents attest to the prices of wooden statuettes, placing such objects at around the average monthly wage in the community (Janssen 1975: 246–8; Weiss 2015: 135). In one example where such transactions are known in some detail (K*RI* VII, 310–11; McDowell 2002: 84–5), the workman Amenemope acquired an image (*twt*) of Seth from the craftsman Merire for a payment in kind totaling a value of two sacks of grain. When he had it brought to the marketplace and showed it to another craftsman, Sawadjit,

Fig. 10 Ostracon with scene of worship, where the workman Khnummose is kneeling before the serpent goddess Meretseger with arms lifted in adoration. British Museum, EA 8510. © Trustees of the British Museum.

the latter appraised it to be worth only half that price. Possibly as a payment for the appraisal, or perhaps as part of a different transaction that led Amenemope to request it in the first place, the note then informs us that Amenemope lent the image to Sawadjit's father for a month. The latter action indicates that such an image could well have a temporary value, possibly lending its powers for a specific purpose, though the text remains silent as to what that might have been.

In discussing this case, Meskell notes the apparent contradiction between divine presence and practical or socio-economic utility, which she suggests must have required people to 'suspend disbelief and the knowledge of human crafting' (Meskell 2004: 104). However, this contradiction (with the insistence on sacred objects as *acheiropoiete*, not made by the hand, e.g. Latour 2002: 18) arises mainly in a context where divinity is transcendent, resulting in an absolute boundary between sacred and profane. In most traditional societies, by contrast, powerful objects tend to be deeply embedded in social life, and may acquire their efficacy because of, not despite, the technical prowess they evidence (cf. Gell 1992). There is nothing in the material examined here that suggests ancient Egypt was any different.

While we thus have ample evidence of private commissioners of images in various contexts, nonetheless the king looms large when it comes to art patronage. Not only did kings commission images of themselves to be erected or carved in their monuments, they also regularly consecrated new images of the gods, and a number of monuments or parts of monuments for private people inform us that they were granted by the king under customs designated as 'favours of the king' (*ḥswt nt ḥr nsw*, cf. Price 2017: 398–9), or with the older designation 'royal gifts' (*ḥtp dì nsw*), the latter of which, however, comes simply to be a general prayer for funerary offerings (cf. e.g Strudwick 2005: 31–2).

Egyptologist Maya Müller has studied the special background and qualifications of the king as commissioner of divine images (Müller 2006). The royal inscriptions of the early second millennium BCE examined by Müller show two basic sources of the king's inspiration for new works of art and architecture. One stems from the king's communion with the gods from whom he can draw direct inspiration, while the other builds on a frequent trope in Egyptian narratives, namely that of discovering authentic and restricted knowledge in ancient manuscripts. Either way, the king relates the revealed 'plans' or 'nature' (the same word *sḫr* encountered in Section 2.1 as designation of a human being's hidden propensities) to his court, so that the work can be realized. In one case, that of the inscription of King Neferhotep (eighteenth century BCE) concerning the rituals at Abydos (Pieper 1929), the inscription even relates that the king himself was personally involved in the manufacturing process in the workshop, possibly not only for ritual efficacy, but also to make sure the image conformed to the specifications that were in this case revealed to the king through an ancient scroll. In a badly preserved inscription, King Akhenaten 400 years later seems to be making a similar instruction to his court, although, in line with the religious reforms of that king, the gist is apparently in this case the inadequacy of traditional cultic images for capturing divine power – though once again, the king has the knowledge required for remedying the situation (Redford 1981).

The interplay between the king as patron and commissioner and the craftsmen is rarely elaborated in such contexts, the focus lying firmly on the role of the king. One stela from the thirteenth century BCE offers an exception to this pattern, by relating a lengthy speech held by King Ramesses II to the craftsmen responsible for the production of two colossal statues of the king (Putter 1997). The speech begins by praising the artisans, 'you valiant men with skillful hands, who hew out monuments for me in any number, who delight in working in valuable stone, skillful with granite, well-versed with quartzite' (K*RI* II, 361, 11–12), etc. The second part of the speech deals in turn with the king's acts as patron of the craftsmen, most notably seeing to their material needs in abundance, for, as the king acknowledges, 'Only on a full stomach does one work on it' (*KRI* II, 362, 3). As ideologically laden as the text is, it confirms some of our reasonable assumptions that often go unexpressed in Egyptian texts, such as the logistic considerations in caring for the significant workforces required for many royal projects. In explicating these considerations, the king's speech echoes much earlier inscriptions detailing private patronage in social life more widely (e.g. Campagno 2014).

The act of commissioning could also go the opposite way, however, from private donor to royal beneficiary. Thus, the scribe Ramose, a prominent member of the Deir el-Medina community, commissioned and donated a shrine set up next to the local temple of Hathor with a cult statue of the reigning king Ramesses II (Haring 1997: 147–8). The inscriptions commemorating this donation specify that the cult was funded by the nearby mortuary temple of the king, though it is unclear whether it was Ramose or the king who in turn covered the temple's expenses, exemplifying the sometimes very convoluted nature of Egyptian cult foundations (Haring 1997, and cf. Spalinger 1985 for an earlier example). It is worth bearing in mind that the commissioning and dedication of a statue would thus usually be accompanied by the establishment of such a foundation or a network of contracts ensuring that the requisite cult would be carried out for the new image. As has been hinted at previously, it is the combination of both statue and cult that ensures the continued presence and accessibility of the ancestor, king, or god worshiped. For the most part, however, we lack the extant written sources of Ramose's case elucidating these concerns.

The final consecration of the statue to make it suitable as a ritual focal point is inextricably connected in the Egyptological literature with a ritual known as the *Opening of the Mouth* (cf. Goyon 1972; Fischer-Elfert 1998; Lorton 1999). The idea that statues had their mouth 'opened' goes back at least to the mid-third millennium BCE, but no details are known about what the ritual entails in relation to statues for most of Egyptian history. Instead it is usually assumed that the acts carried out on statues are identical to a funerary rite of the same name attested from the mid-second millennium onwards, where it is carried out on the mummy of the deceased (Fig. 11), with adaptations for statues of gods in temples known from the mid-first millennium BCE onwards (Cruz-Uribe 1999). This is not an unreasonable conjecture, and evidence like a healing ritual using a smaller figurine indicates that for such images as well, their mouth needed to be opened for them to be able to receive offerings (Roccati 2011: 133, 211–12). However, this example also shows that we probably should not imagine every mention of an 'opening of

Fig. 11 Tomb relief showing the ceremonial purification of the mummy before burial during the *Opening of the Mouth* ritual. Michael C. Carlos Museum, 2001.21.1. © Michael C. Carlos Museum, Emory University. Photo by Bruce M. White, 2015.

the mouth' as implying something like the elaborate funerary rituals depicted on tomb walls. Hence, the idea that any and all statues throughout Egyptian history necessarily had the ritual performed on them precisely as carried out on the mummy during the funeral, and especially that this constituted the crucial transition from an inert object to a ritually charged home for the soul of the deceased, are thus assumptions that go well beyond what can reasonably be deduced from the sources.

Nonetheless, the *Opening of the Mouth* ritual, as known from depictions of funerary rituals, contains a number of allusions to practices and rituals connected to craftsmanship and the production of statuary. Thus, Egyptologist Hans-Werner Fischer-Elfert (1998) has suggested an understanding of some particularly obscure episodes of the ritual carried out on the mummy as references to a vision achieved by a priest of the final image to be carved from the block for the statue. This would add a pivotal element of trance vision to the planning of the statue, perhaps broadly comparable to the king's intuitive grasp of divine imagery as discussed. Proceeding from this interpretation, Fischer-Elfert understands the following series of ritual scenes as a sequential enactment of the production of a statue from the initial vision to the finished sculpture. While these ideas should not be overstated, nor the role and precise contents of the ritual overgeneralized, Fischer-Elfert's interpretation resonates with the close entanglement between craftsmanship and rituals which we will examine from a different perspective in the following section.

3.3 The Aesthetic Dimension

Many Egyptian images evidence a clear focus on the aesthetic dimension. In fact, recent scholars (e.g. Gosden 2001; Winter 2002; Bahrani 2014: 9; Baines 2015: 2–3) have suggested that a concern with aesthetic ordering is the most feasible criterion for – or more useful than – identifying something as 'art' in ancient cultures. But if, as our survey of image terminology and the social settings of images seem to imply, Egyptian conceptions of images involve more than visual attractiveness and conceptual references, what is the role of aesthetics in Egyptian experiences of images?

Here as well, indigenous terminology is a helpful start. Egyptian language contains a few terms that can be approximated by such glosses as 'attractive', 'pleasing', 'beautiful' (Assmann 1988; Schmitz 2006; Semat-Nicoud 2013). Of these, we have already had occasion to explore the meanings of one, namely the root *nfr*, the use of which has been argued, for example, by Müller (1990: 46–7), to indicate a primarily aesthetic sense of beauty in Egyptian culture. As was seen, however, while certainly capable in some contexts of being glossed as 'beautiful', the word *nfr* is significantly broader, and the aesthetic meaning seems to be largely an entailment of the more fundamental ontological sense in which the word denotes a particular status as the embodiment of an ideal (cf. also Widmaier 2017: 131–6 on the cultural specificity of *nfr*).

The other two main candidates for a core vocabulary of aesthetics, the words *ꜥn*, 'beautiful' and *jmꜣ*, 'pleasing' emphasize different aspects of the entity they describe. Both of these words are used mainly of pleasant social relations, where the aesthetic dimension in a narrower sense is not foregrounded.

The word *ꜥn* (with several Semitic cognates) is rare before the fourteenth century BCE, when King Akhentaten revolutionized the worship of the sun god. In this process, the word rose dramatically in prominence to being part of the core vocabulary describing the new solar deity Aten (and more rarely the royal couple as a manifestation of this deity). However, as it is used mainly in laudatory epithets, it is impossible to say whether it refers primarily to the divine grace of the deity, the pleasant and beneficial nature of its manifestation as the visible sun, or its beauty in a more specifically aesthetic sense. A century or so later, in the literary compositions of the Anastasi Papyri, the word is clearly used to describe visually pleasing art and architecture in something approaching a purely aesthetic sense, including a statue (Gardiner 1911: 28, 16–17), and the windows of buildings (Gardiner 1937: 28, 12–13). However, the word retains a number of other usages where the notion of 'beauty' is significantly broader or even metaphorical.

In contrast, the root *jmꜣ* is used from early on to refer to pleasant sensory impressions, although it is not clear that this literal use was ever extended beyond the primary domain of smell. Most likely by metaphorical extension, it is used of gracious social dispositions as a relatively frequent laudatory phrase. Unlike *ꜥn*, however, it does not find use as a general description of aesthetic qualities of artworks or images more specifically.

Other words can be translated as 'adorned', 'embellished', and the like, but here as well, the primary reference of the Egyptian term tends to reside outside the realm of aesthetics properly speaking. For example, the root *mnḫ* is often used of finalizing works of art and architecture, and while this certainly involves an aesthetic dimension in our sense, the core of the Egyptian concept is that of rendering the artifacts 'efficacious' or 'functional' in addition to just 'beautiful'. In fact, the verb is derived from a root designating a 'chisel', and it has been suggested that the extension of its meaning goes through the use of the chisel to prepare mortise and tenon joints, whence the string of linked meanings 'chiseled' -> 'ready for assembly' -> 'ready/suitable for its purpose' -> 'apt, efficacious, efficient' (Lallemand 1922; Westendorf 1973: 137–9; Caritoux 2008: 52).

Perhaps the closest the Egyptian language gets to a term for pure attractiveness and beauty is the root *ḫkr*, translatable as 'to adorn', 'to decorate'. It tends to refer to the use of valuable materials such as silver, gold, or precious stones, as when a stela owner wishes for burial equipment described as 'a coffin of fresh cedar wood, painted and engraved as a masterpiece of the funerary workshop, a mummy case of the choicest gold decorated (*ḫkr*) with real lapis lazuli' (Gayet 1889: pl. 54, l. 9). However, as we have seen, such materials can rarely be reduced to a purely decorative function, and indeed other uses of the word *ḫkr* show that it could certainly be used also to stress cultic efficacy, for example, as a parallel to the word *mnḫ* just discussed in a tomb owner's description of the preparation of his tomb, which is said to be 'equipped with the furnishings of the royal palace, made efficacious (*mnḫ*) with every necessity, filled with decoration (*ḫkr*), equipped with provisions, and furnished with everything that was assigned to it' (*Urk.* VII, 2, 16–20). Thus, while the word *ḫkr* in itself may focus mainly on aesthetic pleasure, in actual usage it is impossible to distinguish this characteristic entirely from that of ritual function.

In a similar way, more detailed concepts such as light and colour are often deeply entangled with concerns of ritual efficacy (e.g. Goebs 2011). Such connections are traditionally interpreted as matters of 'symbolism' where the meaning of each visual element to an audience is thus at issue (e.g. Wilkinson 1994). As will be discussed in Section 3.4, however, the communicative aspects of such uses of light and colour are often negligible in the contexts in which they are deployed. This means that such connections, in line with the fundamental idea of this work presented in the Section 1, are once again better seen as evidence of ontological consubstantiation between the apparently different domains. Thus, in the example mentioned, gold does not symbolize or refer to divinity, but rather the material substance of gold is literally the stuff that gods are made of. Divinity is thus an inherent trait of gold, rather than (or in addition to) being used to make the audience associate whatever is depicted with divinity (cf. the similar approach to materials in Matić 2018). That being so, however, the audience (if any) would certainly have been able to perceive and recognize such material connections, making communicative symbolism a side effect of the properties of the materials.

This brief survey shows that whereas extant Egyptian artworks display a clear concern with aesthetics in our terms, we would err if we understand this as an isolated goal in the Egyptians' own understanding (cf. Müller 1998, for a number of textual examples). Instead, the terminology discussed here indicates that aesthetics was an aspect of the broader functions of images that have been indicated by the discussion of image terminology in the previous sections. Thus, at least as far as the ideology was concerned, beautifying images was not a concern for its own sake, but rather was an intrinsic aspect of ensuring the broader purpose(s) that images were meant to serve – notwithstanding the undeniable fact that many ancient Egyptian objects apparently regarded as fully functional did not succeed entirely in meeting these aesthetic ideals.

A more precise sense of Egyptian aesthetics might be gained, not by looking at the vocabulary, but rather at the artworks produced and appreciated by the Egyptians, and in a sense this is what this work attempts. It is, however, worth noting that it does so from the broader, indigenous viewpoint just presented, in which purely aesthetic concerns cannot easily be disentangled from the other functions and goals of the artwork, but on the contrary can be seen as part and parcel of the fulfillment of these functions and goals (following a position expressed e.g. in Morphy 1989).

This aspect is emphasized by recorded ancient reactions to works of art (cf. Müller 2012). Leaving graffiti in monuments recording one's experience there was an established practice in much of Egyptian history, and such writings can provide important ideas about how the buildings and their decoration were viewed by posterity, often stressing the pleasure with which they were experienced (Hartwig 2004: 43–5; Den Doncker 2010; Verbovsek 2011: 150–1). A collection of such visitors' graffiti comes from rock tombs of the early second millennium BCE evidently visited centuries later, at a time when the cult was no longer performed, and the tomb owners seem to have been long forgotten. Thus, one note following a typical pattern and written on the wall of a tomb at Beni Hasan in Middle Egypt reads, 'He found it like heaven in its interior with the sun shining in it, <and he said, "May heaven rain fresh myrrh> and sprinkle incense upon this temple of that Khufu, true of voice"' (Newberry 1893: pl. 38, no. 3, cf. Spiegelberg 1917: 99). The misunderstanding of the tomb as a temple built by the famous King Khufu likely stems from the fact that the name of this king occurs in the ancient place name for the site, Menat-Khufu. Although clearly literate in the hieratic script in which the graffito is written, the visitor thus seems to have had a limited grasp of the hieroglyphs used in the tomb's inscriptions. In the present connection, it is noteworthy that the immediate reaction to an impressive ancient monument is to wish for cult to be performed there (as evidenced by the wish for myrrh and incense).

This is even clearer in other similar graffiti, such as that of a scribe named Amenemhat who wrote a message praising a tomb of roughly the same age on the west bank of Thebes, describing it as 'pleasant on his heart'. The second half of the graffito is, however, taken up by an offering formula of the type inscribed in funerary monuments dedicated to the owner of the ancient tomb (Davies 1920: pl. 37, no. 33). Effectively, the act of writing a graffito thus becomes a way of resurrecting the long-defunct cult for the tomb owner, emphasizing once again how closely entangled aesthetics and function could be (cf. Quirke 1986: 88), situating the appreciation of art, as Hartwig has aptly noted, at the 'nexus of piety, beauty, and pleasure' (Hartwig 2004: 44).

In a rare example from the seventh century BCE, the owners of two tomb chapels on the western bank of Thebes preempt such reactions by describing in detail the art that can be appreciated inside the tomb chapel, as well as explicitly calling upon visitors to copy the scenes and inscriptions and leave graffiti on its walls (Kuhlmann 1973). The inscription focuses on the evocative quality of the images with accompanying inscriptions that immerse the viewer especially in the soundscape of the depicted scenes, as well as appreciating the variety and accuracy of the images (Jansen-Winkeln 2014: I, 196, 6–9 and II, 640, 10–13):

May you behold the liturgies of the venerable one in their places, with nothing left out. May you hear the quarreling of those talking with their fellows, and may you hear the musicians' songs and the wails of the mourners. May you find the name of each man above him with every job listed, cattle herds, trees and plants with their names above them, with throats moving, the tree in the ground sprouting with branches and fruit, as well as the divine trees of the gods.

Once again, the initial sentence shows that the context of the aesthetic experience is that of the cultic service carried out in the tomb chapel. It is, however, worth noting that the call to appreciate the tomb chapel decoration focuses on the immediate immersive qualities of the scenes, as opposed to separate layers of symbolism or other contextual meanings of the images (cf. e.g. van Walsem 2005: 72–80, for discussion of the question of symbolism in tomb scenes).

3.4 Visible and Invisible Images

The considerations in the previous section regarding the criteria and contexts for the ancient reception of images raises the question of the accessibility of images. This is an unavoidable question for approaches understanding images primarily in terms of communication, and even with the approach taken here, it is important to examine under what conditions images could be encountered. As indicated, the main setting for experiencing images in the temple or tomb was that of the cult directed at, or otherwise surrounded by, those images. This raises questions on the one hand about the audience present on such occasions and the conditions under which images will have been experienced. On the other hand, modes of installation and display also need to be considered, as images were by no means always placed for maximum visibility.

The group of participants in rituals in an elite private tomb was probably always restricted. However, as Hartwig has pointed out, this group would not only have included literate members of the elite, but also, for example, family members who would not have been able to read the inscriptions – and indeed visitors like the aforementioned Amenemhat who could write the hieratic vernacular, but apparently had trouble with hieroglyphs. Along with other indirect evidence, this indicates that reciting (part of) the inscriptions in the tomb may well have formed part of the cultic performance (Hartwig 2004: 47–8). By contrast, temple images, especially the focal cult image kept in the sanctuary of the temple, would have been viewable only by a highly restricted group of specialists, and only within a strictly circumscribed ritual setting (e.g. Baines 1990: 6–7).

To those with access, images and inscriptions would often be poorly lit and inconveniently positioned, for example, for reading texts high on a wall or on the far side of a statue. This is likely true even of statues of private people installed in temples, despite their inscriptions apparently addressing, and promising help to, a larger public (Price 2016). These restricted audiences always posed a problem to approaches emphasizing the role of images (and texts, for that matter) as propaganda, both because of the limited reach and because the precondition for being allowed to view them more or less implied already sharing the ideological message conveyed. However, in a detailed discussion of the sociological implications of secrecy and restricted access, Egyptologist and art historian Christina Riggs has called attention to the effects of such restrictions also on those parts of the 'audience' who were not granted, but might or might not aspire to, access (Riggs 2014: esp. 163–86).

In addition to such restrictions in the audience, the architectural and ritual setting in many cases deliberately obstructed the clear viewing of images. With the exception of depictions on the entrance pylons and walls of the open courts of temples, most tomb and temple images would be viewed indoors, in many cases depending solely on the light source brought by visitors. A particularly instructive phenomenon in this regard is the architectural feature of many tombs of the third millennium BCE known as the *serdab* (Arabic for 'cellar'). The *serdab* is a separate room next to the cult chapel, which is either completely walled off from the latter, or accessible only through a small slit or window (Lehmann 2000). The statue(s) of the tomb owner were deposited in the *serdab* where they were thus able to function as one of the primary focal points for the cult, and were able, for example, to benefit from the incense burned in chapel, yet with the limited viewing and lighting conditions would have remained largely unseen (Fig. 12).

Depositing statues in *serdabs* is a clear sign that uninhibited visibility of the kind we associate with ancient artifacts through practices of museum display was not a primary aim for ancient Egyptian images. We may immediately think of practices of illusion, where restricted visibility can enhance the mimetic effect by which the image can be mistaken for reality. This idea is corroborated by the Orientalist trope of the impressionable and superstitious Oriental, as perpetuated, for example, in the anecdote of an indigenous workman who was struck with fear when he broke through the wall to the chamber containing the life-like statues of Rahotep and Nefret (Daninos 1886: 71). This story is repeated frequently in popular works as one of the key facts about these famous works of sculpture, often 'improved' to have not just one, but numerous, if not all, of the workmen fleeing in terror (e.g. Silverman 2003: 201; el-Shahawy 2005: 71. In Reeves 2001: 58, there is still just one workman, but he is now 'jabbering incoherently' for dramatic effect when coming out of the tomb).

Fig. 12 Painted limestone statue of Sames as deposited in the serdab of his tomb at Giza (G 1104h), July 1904. A10881_OS. Photograph © 2020 Museum of Fine Arts, Boston.

However, it is worth remembering that the very distinction between reality and illusion is part and parcel of the representationalist framework, so that in order to approximate the ancient experience we may have to find a way to suspend it conceptually (cf. Bahrani 2003: 122–3). The phenomenological idea that the visible is always only a partial manifestation of the invisible may offer an alternative to (or a more specifically relevant aspect of) the notion of illusionism. Along these lines, I have suggested elsewhere that this manner of highly restrictive display elicits a special experience of the presence of the ancestor as *felt* and *known*, rather than strictly *seen* (Nyord 2013a; cf. also Nyord 2013b; frequent parallels elsewhere, e.g. the notion of *praesentia* in Brown 1981).

The deliberate restriction of viewing the statue in the *serdab*, not to mention the frequent deposition of images in completely sealed-off burial chambers, thus indicates that we may go astray if we insist on images as a purely visual phenomenon. Discussions of ancient Egyptian images have often assumed more or less implicitly that an image requires a viewer (e.g. Müller 2006: 28; cf. Geimer 2007, for the question in art history more generally). Sometimes this is taken to the point where images that were clearly made or deposited in such a way as to make them completely invisible must then be understood to be made for the viewing of the gods or the dead to secure this apparently fundamental aspect of the image (e.g. Baines 2015: 16). Beyond its clearly ad hoc nature, there is no strict argument against such an idea of panoptic viewers, and in late texts we do find expressions of the idea that gods descend to 'see' their images before eventually 'joining' with them (e.g. Kurth 1998: 80–8). In the view argued here, where aspects of images such as iconography are viewed as a capturing of powers in material form, rather than primarily as messages to be decoded and/or appreciated, there is no particular need always to have a visual audience for an image – even if many Egyptian images clearly were made with an audience in mind. Instead, the notion of the audience becomes much broader, to include also the people remembering, guessing, knowing about, or half-sensing through flickering shadows and whiffs of incense, the presence of the image.

A final consideration should be discussed at this point, namely that of ancient Egyptian notions of veiling and hiding as a matter of deeper import than a pure focus on visibility might indicate. Christina Riggs (2014: 94–108) has recently called attention to the apparently widespread, but largely overlooked, practice of wrapping images prior to deposition (Fig. 13), which she understands as a transformative process relating 'not to the human we might think we see, but rather to the divine we cannot grasp' (Riggs 2014: 108). A closely associated aspect was explored in an earlier paper by Ragnhild Bjerre Finnestad (Finnestad 1989), where she notes that what is effectively meant by expressions of 'hiding' in religious texts is actually closer to notions of 'latent' or 'potential life'. Thus, in Egyptian religious thought being 'secret' or 'hidden' does not simply mean being temporarily or permanently out of sight, but rather it is a separate mode of existence in which the 'hidden' has not (yet) acquired the precise contours

Fig. 13 Figurines wrapped in linen from the tomb of Tutankhamun demonstrating that unrestricted visibility was not the main concern for Egyptian images. Griffith Institute, Burton Photograph No. P1949. Reproduced with permission of Griffith Institute, University of Oxford.

characterizing full existence. Once again, then, we see the all-important onto-logical principle of emergence at work, in which wrapping, burying, and sealing away an entity does not merely hide it from view but confers upon it the primeval, not (yet) fully differentiated mode of existence assimilating it to the Nile flood, the night, and the immanent but hidden god or ancestor.

3.5 Affects of images

A significant challenge in recent thinking about object ontologies in archae-ology and anthropology is that of grasping the effect of individual design choices for the ontological status of the object (cf. Robb 2015). As has been seen throughout this section, it is possible to understand both the overall status of being an image and the use of materials in the ontological key espoused here. This raises the question whether it is possible to transpose more detailed design choices traditionally understood mainly as communicative features, such as style and iconography, in a similar way.

We have already encountered the idea of shaping and painting as ways of eliciting and fixing particular powers inhering in the material. On this view, iconography (e.g. of kingship), becomes less a matter of transmitting a message about identity (although it can be used for this purpose as well) and more about drawing out the ontological intersection between features of a rock and divine kingship, in order ultimately to effect the higher-level connection between the image and the person it depicts (see Section 2).

However, images of a given entity could evidently be fashioned in a number of different ways while retaining this general connection between depiction and depicted (cf. e.g. Connor 2016–2017). This indicates that such design choices could alter the specific features of how the depicted entity was made manifest in a given connection, as well as changing the relationship to other powers more or less integral to that entity. For example, a king would almost always be depicted showing one or more elements of royal iconography, not (just) to show viewers that he was a king, but to make sure that the presence effected by the image was of the depicted person *as* a king. The concept of affects introduced in Section 1 is useful here. Anthropologist Eduardo Viveiros de Castro has aptly characterized the human body as 'a bundle of affects' (Viveiros de Castro 2015: 109), empha-sizing the capacity of such affects to enter or leave the 'bundle'; for example, as the body changes from one shape to another. This is a helpful perspective for understanding the role of images created for a particular context in ancient Egypt as well. What is conventionally regarded as iconography used to send a message, on this view, becomes ways of eliciting specific affects in the material. This can be seen especially clearly with objects like amulets (Fig. 14), which often show

Fig. 14 As a concretion of solar and divine powers, gold was a valued material for powerful objects, as in this gold foil amulet of a scarab, the hieroglyph for the verb *ḫpr*, 'to become, to emerge'. Michael C. Carlos Museum, 1921.192. © Michael C. Carlos Museum, Emory University. Photo by Peter Harholdt.

strong preference for particular combinations of iconography and materials, both in the written instructions for making them and as they are actually found in the archaeological record (Andrews 1994; Dubiel 2008: 59–63).

The precise material, posture, and features of an image thus had to be adequate, not merely for the depicted entity, but also for the context in which the image was to effect its presence. While the details of these considerations are naturally lost to us today, it is likely that archaeologically attested patterns, such as the preference for particular statue types in specific contexts, is a sign of this type of consideration. For example, the type of so-called block statues (Fig. 15) used exclusively to effect the presence of non-royal humans in contexts where they were not actively involved in the rituals as either ritualist or recipient. This function is consonant not only with the resting posture (Schulz 1992; Schulz 2011), but also with the largely hidden body understood along the lines of the emergence principle discussed previously as embodying a withdrawn, partly potential mode of existence and presence.

Fig. 15 Block statue of Djedkhonsuefankh showing the owner in an emergent
state of embodiment. Metropolitan Museum of Art, 07.228.27.

In a few cases, such attention to the context and relationships of the image is
explicitly brought out in inscriptions. For example, a statue of King Thutmose
III embodied as a Nile God holding an offering table with foodstuffs and flowers
carries the inscription, 'An image (*twt*) of Menkheperre [Thutmose III] bringing
fresh produce (*rnpt*) to Amun in Ipet-Sut' (*Urk.* IV, 885, 14). This inscription
confirms what we might already have deduced from a visual examination,
namely that the statue was designed for a specific contextual purpose, and that
the image was conceived of as being not just of the king in general, but of the
king carrying out this specific action.

As noted, one way to think about images in ancient Egypt is as objects
adequate for the embodiment of a particular entity. Correspondingly,
a number of steps were taken to ensure this crucial general connection. Many
of these may well have been part of social convention that is now lost, or simply
the deposition of a statue in the tomb of a particular person. More visible today
is the act of inscribing images with the name of the person depicted. The fact

that this is often the main way today in which we can attribute an image to a specific person may tempt us to overemphasize this aspect. However, the inscribed name as a permanent way of establishing the connection between an entity and its image was frequently stressed by the ancient Egyptians as well, as when a wish inscribed on a statue reads, 'May my name remain on this statue of mine without disappearing for posterity' (K*RI* III, 69, 12–13).

4 What Can an Image Do?

It was suggested at the beginning of this work that what looks to us at first sight like referential and symbolic connections can more fruitfully be regarded as ontological entanglement when attempting to understand ancient Egyptian images. In the preceding sections, we have examined various aspects of what this might entail in practice, both from the perspective of the kind of connections posited by the indigenous terminology, and by looking at the wider cultural frameworks of imaging practices. In this section, we will complement this picture by examining some salient examples of actual ancient Egyptian uses of images.

One way to categorize uses of images is according to the kind of relationships they posit between the image and the depicted entity (Nyord 2017). The first type of usage can be labeled 'presentification' (a term coined by Vernant 1991: 151–63 for ancient Greek images) and entails the ontological connection between image and person being used to allow the former to function as a manifestation of the latter. The typical example is the cult statue of a god or deceased person enabling ritual interaction, but the living could also be similarly presentified. More complex uses could set up configurations between multiple images or other presentifications such as inscribed names, metaphorical or metonymic objects, or the mummy of the deceased in the tomb chamber.

The second type of connection is meant to induce changes or otherwise influence the entity depicted through the making and/or subsequent manipulation of the image. If the presentifying image is thus characterized by a main direction of attention and influence from the entity to the image, altering images works mostly the opposite way. In this case, it is the mode of depiction, the place of deposition, and/or the ritual manipulation of the image that can end up influencing the depicted entity.

The third and final type is rare in ancient Egypt, and unlike the other two, it posits only a temporary connection between image and entity which can later be severed. In Egypt, this type of connection typically allows adverse effects such as illness or haunting to be transferred from a person to an image. When the image is subsequently broken or the connection is otherwise severed, the person becomes freed from whatever effect was transferred to the image.

Fig. 16 The tomb owner presentified before the table of offerings, providing a matrix for the cultic acts to be carried out in the tomb. Michael C. Carlos Museum, 2008.59.1B. © Michael C. Carlos Museum, Emory University. Photo by Bruce M. White, 2011.

As all of these uses of images are based on the same fundamental kind of ontological connection, the categories are not mutually exclusive, but are rather a matter of the main focus a given practice takes. Thus, it is possible for the same kind of object to shift gradually from one of the categories to another over time, as seems to be the case with the *shabti* figurines discussed in Section 4.3.

It is also possible for people subsequently to put an image to a different use than what was first intended, causing the focal type of connection to shift. This is the topic for Section 4.4, which deals with such examples of this as iconoclasm where an originally presentifying image is used subsequently to harm the depicted person, essentially reversing the focal direction of influence.

4.1 Image as Material Presence

The notion that an image can be used to establish the material presence of the entity depicted will be very familiar through the discussion and examples in previous sections. For both the gods and the dead, presentifying images formed one of the main focal points of the regular cult. As such, the presence of the statue becomes pivotal to the general function of the tomb and temple.

In one of the most detailed relatively recent discussions of ancient Egyptian cult images, Lorton characterized the basic 'problem' that Egyptian rituals meant to address as being 'that of an inert material substrate that had to be enlivened and then tended with ritual and offerings' (Lorton 1999: 133). As the wording shows, much of the thinking about ancient Egyptian images and their function has been predicated on a stark dualism between inert material on the one hand and the presence of sentient beings such as gods and ancestors on the other.

As we have seen in the previous sections, we probably come closer to the Egyptian way of thinking if we consider different kinds of powers as always inhering more or less manifestly in materials, at least the ones that the Egyptians used for images. On this view, the function of the cult would not be that of summoning an extraneous spirit into the otherwise inert matter, but would rather be a question of heightening the intensity of the presence inhering in the object by virtue of its material, shape, locality, and other connections. Such a heightened intensity of material presence may in fact be what the Egyptians designated with the central religious term *ḥtp* – the effect of offerings on the recipient, conventionally rendered simply as 'satisfied, peaceful, resting' (Lekov 2005: 22–4, has even suggested an understanding as 'merging' in such cases).

More exceptionally, encounters with images may also take place spontaneously outside the cultic setting. One such experience relates to the sphinx at Giza, which, more than a millennium after its construction, had become covered with sand. The prince who was later to become King Thutmose IV in the early fourteenth century BCE was hunting at the ancient cemetery, and as he rested near the buried sphinx, the god Harakhte (whom the sphinx was understood to depict) spoke to him. The god asked him to clear the sand covering the monument, and promised that if he did so, he would become king. All of this happened as promised, and the king commissioned a stela to commemorate the event, which now stands between the front paws of the sphinx (*Urk.* IV, 1539–1544). The main interest in this narrative from the present perspective is the double directionality of connections enabled by the sphinx as image: proximity to the sphinx was what predicated the encounter with the god, while in turn the god had a keen interest in the conditions of his image as one aspect of his bodily presence in the world.

While the specific cultic availability offered by presentifying images is clearly of pivotal importance, there are a number of other implications of presence in a given place as well. Particularly worthy of notice are the multiple ways in which images can be configured in relation to each other in order to elicit or materialize relationships between the entities depicted. The simplest instance of this is setting up a single image in a place intrinsically connected with another entity. Thus, a sandstone statue of a man named Iri from the mid-first millennium BCE states this idea plainly with the inscription, 'I placed this statue in the temple, so that I would never be far from it' (Borchardt 1934: 60).

Occasionally, the aspect of spatial proximity and presence is overridden by the general relationship between the image and its human user. Thus, an ostracon from Deir el-Medina reveals the consternation of a former owner of what is presumably some kind of image (Černý 1939: pl. 3, no. 251): 'Please make me a *wrt*-image(?), for the one you had made for me has been stolen away. Thus, it might work a manifestation of Seth against me'. Although the exact nature of the object is unfortunately obscure – the word means simply 'a great one', while the writing indicates a type of goddess – the reference to a 'manifestation of Seth' shows the writer's anxiousness that its loss may lead to adverse effects (Borghouts 1982: 15–19). Seth is a strong, but chaotic and unpredictable god, and in personal matters is often associated with illness and other threats to one's fortune and well-being. The relational character of the object is clear here: Its loss represents a rupture of relations between the owner and the object's power. While presence and proximity is beneficent, absence can be dangerous, as the connection between image and owner remains even when the object is lost, though it thus changes its character. Apparently, acquiring a new object of the same type as the one that was lost would avert the danger.

By adding additional images, the complexity of configurations can become considerable. This is particularly true of funerary assemblages, where numerous texts, images, and image-like objects making similar use of materials and iconography can surround the body of the deceased. Many such objects across shifting burial customs focus on establishing a situation where the deceased body is surrounded by gods and protective beings. This configuration draws both on the mythological idea of the protection of the dead god Osiris by other gods, and on the ritual wake before the funeral where this situation is enacted (see e.g. the decoration of coffins of the early second millennium BCE, cf. Willems 1988; Nyord 2014).

An example of such a funerary configuration is the use of bricks with painted or sculpted images inserted into the walls of burial chambers of the fifteenth century BCE and later (Lüscher 1998: 54–7; Régen 2010). The images are identifiable as ritual and mythological iconography, such as the $ḏd$-pillar representing the backbone of Osiris, a torch of the kind used in the wake, and an image of the funerary god Anubis (Fig. 17). These images were then inserted into niches in the wall of the burial chamber, so that they surrounded the body of the deceased in each of the cardinal directions. A text from the Book of the Dead related to this practice shows that the underlying idea is that of transforming the burial chamber into that of the god Osiris by re-establishing the divine relationships present there (chapter 151; see Lüscher 1998). Characteristically, the way to make the deceased take on the ritual role of Osiris is by spatially configuring the relationships between that god and the other deities present in the mythological scenario.

Many of the two-dimensional images on the walls of tombs and temples can be understood similarly as ways of establishing (and displaying) relations between the depicted entities. This is most obviously the case with depictions of rituals for the god and the tomb owner of the kind that would actually be performed there, where the image serves to elicit and make permanent the relationship between ritualist(s) and beneficiary that carrying out the ritual would entail. Apart from ritual scenes, much of the traditional wall decoration of private tomb chapels concerns the so-called 'viewing'-scenes, where an oversized tomb owner views, and often acts as the centre of attention for, people carrying out a wide range of activities (cf. e.g. van Walsem 2005: 33–9). From the perspective taken here, such scenes would serve to establish the depicted relationship between the tomb owner and the work processes, which are perhaps best understood (and sometimes explicitly identified) as taking place in the funerary domain established by the tomb owner to take care of the cult. It is worth noting, however, that by the logic of presentifying images such a connection would go both ways, so that not only does the tomb owner benefit from the activities because of the cult, but the many people whose livelihood the foundation provides are in turn working under the beneficent gaze of the tomb owner.

Fig. 17 Configurations of images could create powerful spaces. Four bricks with three-dimensional images for insertion in the walls of the burial chamber. British Museum, EA 41544–41547. © Trustees of the British Museum.

Presentifying imagery was thus most likely significantly more widespread than the clear and specific case of cult statues. Many emblematic representations of kings and other owners of monuments can be understood in a broadly similar way as not only displaying, but also establishing, ligatures between the depicted entities. A good example is the so-called *sm3-t3wy* ('unification of the Two Lands') motif often found on thrones and other pieces of royal display (Fig. 18). Known since the Early Dynastic period in the early third millennium, the motif shows the tying together of two heraldic plants, respectively emblematic of Upper and Lower Egypt with the hieroglyph for the word *sm3*, 'unify' in the middle (e.g. Fitzenreiter 2011). In this configuration, the papyrus plant embodies Lower Egypt, while a less certainly identifiable plant (cf. e.g. Desroches-Noblecourt 1995: 58–74), conventionally understood as a water lily, but looking quite different from the typical iconography of this plant and perhaps more likely to be a sedge (Gay Robins, personal communication), embodies Upper Egypt. Often, as in the example reproduced here, the stalks of the two plants are held by two corpulent fecundity figures embodying the fertility of the river Nile, or else by another pair of deities standing for Upper and Lower Egypt, such as Horus and Seth.

In purely communicative terms, this can be understood as a propagandistic display of the king's claim to rulership. Since the earliest history of Egyptian kingship, the country was regarded as inherently or potentially fragmented, so that the act of unifying the land under a single ruler was seen ideologically as one of the main feats of the reigning king, even in times of the utmost political stability. At the same time, the motif communicates another core tenet of Egyptian royal ideology, namely that of rule by divine sanction – it is not the king himself, but rather the central divinities associated with the land and its prosperity who carry out the act of uniting. As such, the motif becomes a salient

Fig. 18 Emblematic unification of the Two Lands, with Lower Egypt on the right and Upper Egypt on the left, from the base of a colossal statue of King Ramesses II (whose names above the 'unification' hieroglyph are omitted here) in the Luxor Temple. Line drawing by Henrijette Vex Nyord.

expression of some of the most central ideas about the king's role in the Egyptian cosmos.

Understanding the use of such motifs (also) as an example of presentifying images makes it easier to explain the way they were used by the Egyptians (cf. also Baines 1985: 239). In this case, the motif aims not so much at being 'read', understood, and accepted by an audience, but rather works by itself to establish the configuration depicted in the material on which it is made. Thus, the images of plants and deities can be seen as manifestations of the powers and affects dwelling in what is depicted. The image of the tying together of the plant stalks, then, is neither a representation of an actual act taking place elsewhere, nor a metaphorical reference to the political reality of rulership. Rather, it is itself an act of tying together the powers inherent in the two plant species – powers evidenced, among many other ways, by their capacity to embody the two parts of Egypt in representations like these.

By deploying this motif on a concrete object, the configuration becomes part of a larger assemblage, where it is entangled with further persons, places, and imagery. In the case of the royal statue, the image of the king often sits supported by this motif, so that he is, in a concretely embodied sense, upheld by the process effected by the image.

While the *smꜣ-tꜣwy* motif usually retains its reference to, or association with, a specific king either through text or image, other configurations of iconography stand more on their own, making it possible for the powerful object carrying them to be used in a variety of ways. A good example of this is the category of faience bowls from the mid-second millennium known as 'marsh bowls' because of their predominant decoration with motifs of flora and fauna from Egyptian marsh and river landscapes (Krönig 1934; Strauss 1974; Milward 1982; Tschorn 2017: 435–6). Most often, the inside of such bowls show a centrifugal scheme in the decoration, where different floral and faunal elements emerge from the centre of the bowl. The centre contains a square structure, sometimes marked by iconography identifying it as a pool of water, although often this is abstracted to consist of geometric (square or triangular) fields of alternating black and blue colour (Fig. 19).

The water lily ('lotus') plays a particularly important role in the decoration of the bowls, both on the inside where they are the most frequent plant emerging from the centre of the bowl, and on the outside, which is often decorated in a way assimilating the shape of the bowl as a whole to the flower. Buds of the white water lily in nature open in the morning and close again in the afternoon, thereby seemingly mirroring the diurnal cycle of the sun (e.g. Pommerening, Marinova, and Hendrickx 2010: 14–15). Along with their emerging from, and floating on, the surface of water, this gave strong associations with the Egyptian

Fig. 19 Marsh bowl with centrifugal plant design around a central rectangular pool. Metropolitan Museum of Art, 26.7.905.

concept of creation as emergence from a hidden, potential state. For this reason, water lilies figure prominently in Egyptian art and mythology.

The second most frequent motif on the marsh bowls, that of the Nile *tilapia* (Fig. 20), once again resonates with the concept and experience of creation by emergence. The *tilapia* is a mouthbrooder, and the female of the species keeps the fertilized eggs in her mouth until they hatch, and can subsequently take the fry back into her mouth for protection. The result is a striking instance of the emergence principle: The adult fish lets out a swarm of smaller-scale copies of itself that were previously kept invisibly within the confines of its body. The Egyptians may well have further observed that this process is cyclical in that the mother periodically lets the fry back into its mouth, which would only have added to the potency of the fish's embodiment of this ontological principle.

The two motifs are often combined in a way not found in nature, but which underscores their conceptual compatibility. Instead of the lotus emerging from the water, and the *tilapia* fry emerging from the mouth of their mother, the lotus may be shown as emerging from the mouth of the *tilapia* (Fig. 20). The theme of actualization through emergence is found also at the level of the larger composition. The centre of the bowl is not only the point of emergence for the lotus, but also the static centre in the many compositions where the dynamic nature of the more peripheral areas is stressed through patterns of circular or centrifugal movement. At the same time, while the central field is often abstracted to pure geometric forms, the peripheral area is characterized by details determining individual plant and animal species. This contrast once again mirrors that between primeval unity on the one hand and the differentiated multiplicity of the created world on the other.

These conceptual schemes in the painted decoration are supported by the material of the bowls. The shining blue colour of the faience is particularly apt for the depiction of the aquatic marsh environment, but the conceptual affordances of the efflorescence technique resonates in particular with the emergence principle as stressed by the painted decoration. As was seen in Section 3.1, Egyptian faience creates an ambiguous relationship between the internal and the external by capturing an ongoing process of emergence in a way that cannot be resolved conclusively (Nyord 2020).

The same set of concepts and experiences is thus deliberately evoked at each of the different levels of material, iconography, and overall composition. In line with the ideas on presentification outlined, the blue colour that gradually emerges from the faience paste as it dries does not refer to or represent water, but it 'leads' the same ontological process which results elsewhere in water. The painted patterns of fish and lily buds similarly work to draw the processes out of

Fig. 20 The *tilapia*-fish embodying the creative powers of marshland and Nile water features prominently in faience 'marsh bowls'. The Walters Art Museum, 48.400.

the material that result in the becoming of these entities in 'nature'. The fact that these patterns occur here as manganese paint on faience paste given regular shape using a clay mould offers entirely new possibilities for recombining these ontological vectors in ways not found in nature, as seen most characteristically with the frequent motif of the water lily bud emerging from the mouth of the *tilapia* (Fig. 20). Here, the blooming of the lily bud emerging from the water and the fractal self-duplication of the fish from its mouth are what we would label natural phenomena, but their principled combination can only occur in a painting, not in nature.

What may the purpose of such an object be? In light of the ontological roles and terminology of images examined so far, we can hypothesize that the fusion of the aquatic environment with the material serves less to depict the real Nile or marshes and more to actualize the processes of creation by emergence which are also found there, in new contexts and new combinations enabled by the affordances of the material. We would expect such a concretion of the creative powers of the Nile and marsh environments to be broadly useful across a range of cultural domains, and indeed 'marsh bowls' have been found not only as funerary equipment (e.g. Hayes 1935), but also as votive offerings to the goddess Hathor (Pinch 1993: 308–15), as well as in domestic settings (Nicholson 1998: 56–63).

It is worth noting at the end of this discussion that there is no necessary contradiction between communicative and presentifying imagery. The dichotomy arises mainly from the fact that only the communicative use is admitted by representationalist intuitions, which can make it seem as if the two are mutually exclusive, so that we have to label apparently exceptional cases as 'apotropaic', 'protective', or simply 'symbolic'. If the representationalist expectations are abandoned, both functions can easily be understood as being simultaneously active in one and the same image. In this case, the prominence with which the image is displayed, and the audience to which it was made accessible, will often be the best guides as to the relative importance of the two aspects to the ancient actor.

4.2 Images Inducing Changes

If the primary focus of presentifying images is thus to effect the material presence of a being in a particular time, place, and manner, what I have termed altering images have their main emphasis on the latter of these aspects. As seen in the previous sections, presentifying images tend to be idealizing and stereotyping, and altering images take this tendency to its logical extreme by employing often explicitly counterfactual depictions. The basic function is, however, the exact same, so that presentification and alteration are simply opposite ends of a continuum. Thus, depicting a being in a particular manner is here also a way of establishing the affects depicted. This was referred to previously as enabling the depicted being to play a particular role in a given time and place, but in this case the 'role' gets an even broader sense than such examples as 'recipient of offerings' or 'smiter of enemies'.

Because they are less contextually bound than presentifying images, altering images can be more difficult to recognize. To show the range of functions of such images, we will look at two groups of objects where this function is clearly attested, conventionally known as fertility figurines and execration figures, respectively.

Female figurines in different materials are found throughout ancient Egyptian history (Waraksa 2008). While the traditional notion that all such figurines are necessarily meant to further fertility can be questioned (e.g. Waraksa 2009), inscriptions on a few such figurines make the purpose of at least those exemplars clear: to help a woman conceive a child (Nyord 2017). Figurines of this category show a naked woman carrying a child on her hip (Fig. 21). The figurine can thus be understood as a depiction of the woman for whom a child is wished,

Fig. 21 Painted limestone figurine of woman holding a child. Metropolitan Museum of Art, 22.2.34.

while the situation depicted of carrying a child is the one to be effected by the figurine.

The role of the figurine in this case is thus that of bringing certain potentials inherent in the woman to actualization. This is basically similar to the function of presentifying images, which, as seen in the previous section, relies on features like posture and iconography to create an embodiment adequate for a given entity in a given context. However, the focus in this case is not that of making the woman present for interaction, but rather the figurine is meant to induce the change depicted in the flesh-and-blood body of the woman.

The relational function of the image remains in such cases as well, however. The ability to give birth is understood to depend on the prospective parent's ancestor, so that the figurines were placed as votive gifts in a tomb. This means that the figurines would also have a presentifying function fundamentally akin to the placement of a statue of a private person in a temple to elicit a relationship to the entity present in the cult place.

A different, essentially hostile, situation is found with the so-called execration figures. This is a group of related materials including not only figurines, but also pottery inscribed with names of enemies (discussion in Ritner 1993: 136–80; overview of material in Theis 2014: 708–31). During the third and early second millennium, assemblages of such material were deposited in necropoleis in various places in Egypt. The most detailed figurines show a kneeling, bound prisoner, whose body has been smoothed to make a surface for the lengthy inscription. Other examples can be seen as abstracted versions of this shape, sometimes to the point of becoming merely flat tags with an indication of a head and a brief inscription (Fig. 22). Versions of the same inscription were also written on pottery, which was broken as part of the ritual.

The fullest versions of the inscription found on a group of pots now in Berlin (Sethe 1926) lists named foreign rulers along with generic designations such as 'their champions, their runners, their confederates, their allies', grouped according to the general directions in which they lived, and ending with possible internal enemies in Egypt, deceased Egyptians, and general phenomena such as slander or bad dreams. When inscribed on a figurine, the object thus becomes identified with this lengthy list of beings, all of whom become in a sense

Fig. 22 Figure of bound enemy stylized to form a label allowing the identification in red ink of the targeted enemy. Metropolitan Museum of Art, 33.1.97.

'depicted' and thus embodied by the object, even though some of them are apparently purely potential, such as everyone 'who will rebel, who will plot, who will fight, who say they will fight, who say they will rebel'. As we have seen, a broad conceptual adequacy is more important than likeness, and a figurine of a prisoner capable of relating to a whole range of actual and imagined people at once is a good example of this, with a pot inscribed with the same list being an even more extreme case where even the generic notion of 'likeness' missing. Rather, in both cases the affordance of breakability seems paramount, both for the adequacy of the 'image', and for its suitability for the ritual.

During the ritual in which they were deposited, the objects were often broken or put in a jar before being buried (e.g. Osing 1976). A particularly elaborate case from the Nubian site of Mirgissa involves not only the breaking of figurines and pottery, but also the burning of wax objects (presumably images), and a human sacrifice (Vila 1973; Ritner 1993: 153–5).

In contrast to the fertility figurines, where the desired effect is relatively straightforward, it is more difficult to see precisely what the execration rituals were meant to accomplish, with scholarly suggestions ranging from the 'ultimate death' (Ritner 2012: 395) of the enemies whose images were destroyed to a purely psychological effect giving an edge in actual battle against them (Quack 2002: 156). From the perspective of the logic of the image, we can suggest two interrelated stages. The first is the embodiment of the depicted person in the image. As with the fertility figurines, this involves presentification with the specific affects of a bound prisoner, aimed at actualizing the potential of the depicted person to enter this role. The second stage, that of breaking the image, is related to the 'iconoclastic' treatment of images to be discussed in Section 4.4. The range of treatments of breaking, burying, and burning images suggest that Ritner is right in seeing this basically as an execution in effigy (Ritner 2012). On analogy with the fertility figurine, we should most likely see this as a manipulation of the underlying 'analogistic' connections between things, rather than a pseudo-causal act that automatically makes the depicted person drop dead (as in the popular notion of the 'voodoo doll' often invoked in this connection, e.g. Ritner 1993: 112–13).

As with the presentifying use of images, it is worthwhile in this case as well to distinguish between the non-representational reading espoused here and a purely representational one. It is clear that the imagery used to depict foreigners would, in principle, serve to express and entrench certain ideologically charged views of foreigners. In this sense, the images could be seen as political expressions about the nature and roles of the foreign peoples depicted. While the small scale, often abstract nature and manner of deposition (mostly burial in an old graveyard) makes this unlikely to be a main concern in the case of the execration figures, other similar imagery was often prominently displayed on temples and other monuments, both royal and private (Bestock 2018).

By contrast, because it is difficult to imagine a properly communicative function of fertility figurines, they have usually been regarded as straight-forwardly 'magical', although certainly they could similarly be seen as a way of materializing (and thus communicating, albeit presumably to a very small audience) the Egyptian ideal of engendering heirs and the pressures upon, perhaps especially, women to realize this ideal.

4.3 Images as Substitute Bodies

Images for substitution are much rarer in ancient Egyptian ritual practice than either of the two previous categories. Based once again on the fundamental experience of an ontological ligature between depiction and depicted, images for substitution work in two stages. The first is very similar to that of presentify-ing images in establishing a bond of mutual influence between the two. The second stage is what sets this use of images apart, in that the bond is deliberately broken subsequently, so that adverse effects that actually or poten-tially affected the depicted person become insulated to affect only the image.

As with other uses of images, substitution may have been more widespread than indicated in the extant sources, but in terms of strictly explicit occurrences, this use of images is found only in a few healing rituals where an illness can be transferred to a figurine. A clear example comes from a ritual manuscript written in the late thirteenth or early twelfth century BCE (though the rites recorded in it will have been, perhaps significantly, older). The rite in question is for curing bellyache and consists of an incantation assimilating the patient with the sun god Re, who is cured of a similar ailment in the mythic narrative (recent discussion in Waraksa 2009: 148–54). The instruction following the incantation tells the user to recite it 'over a female figure of clay. As for any suffering in the belly, the affliction upon him [sc. the patient] will enter the female figure of Isis, so that he becomes healthy' (Borghouts 1971: 25 and pl. 12).

Once again, the logic underlying this ritual is relational. The figurine does not represent the patient him- or herself, but rather the goddess Isis. In the myth to which the incantation alludes, Isis is herself secretly responsible for the sun god's illness, and extorts him to tell her his secret name, explaining that only in this way will she be able to heal him (cf. Borghouts 2008). By using a figurine of Isis, the material component of the ritual thus serves to establish the same relational pattern as that related verbally in the recitation. According to the ritual instructions, instantiating this pattern makes it possible for the illness to be absorbed in the figurine, after which the temporary relationship established by the ritual can be dissolved.

A popular notion in modern Egyptology of the image as substitute is that of the funerary figurines known as *shabtis* (Fig. 23). Conventional wisdom has it that the Egyptians believed the dead could be called upon to carry out corvee labour in the beyond, and that *shabti* figurines were deposited in tombs, so that they could carry out the work in his or her place, leaving the deceased free to enjoy the afterlife. However, there are a few problems with this understanding, especially as far as

Fig. 23 The typical image for substitution in ancient Egypt, according to its inscription the *shabti* was made explicitly for carrying out 'work' on behalf of its owner. Michael C. Carlos Museum, 1998.11. © Michael C. Carlos Museum, Emory University. Photo by Peter Harholdt.

the earlier uses of *shabtis* are concerned (see Nyord 2018b: 75–6). The earliest examples of *shabti* figurines seem not to have been used in this way, but rather to have been deposited in powerful places where the depicted person was not actually buried – in other words, a clear matter of presentification. This indicates that the work alluded to in the *shabti* inscription was not originally thought of as an onerous duty to be avoided, but, on the contrary, formed part of the relations that the deposition of the figurine sought to establish. Given the framework developed in Section 4.1, this 'work' would then likely refer to ritual duties, and in fact Egyptologist Christiane Desroches-Noblecourt has suggested an interpretation where *shabtis* serve precisely to multiply the agency of their owner to allow a complete embedding in the regenerative cycles of the cosmos (Desroches-Noblecourt 1995: 157–67) – a notion in much better consort with the rest of our knowledge of Egyptian mortuary thought. Perhaps, then, the *shabtis* were not thought to free the deceased of the burden of irksome afterlife duties, and thus function as substitutes in the sense discussed here, at all (or only as a relatively late further development)?

4.4 Changes of Images

The three categories discussed so far cover the main purposes for which the great majority of Egyptian images were first made. However, a vast number of artworks from ancient Egypt bear evidence of subsequent reuse or manipulation, often in ways that change the original relationships that the image configured. The most widespread examples of such subsequent manipulations are, on the one hand, 'iconoclasm' in which images are deliberately damaged, sometimes in very specific ways, and, on the other hand, patterns of reuse, where objects are reworked and/or re-inscribed to benefit an owner different from the one for whom the object was first intended.

The focus on images as ways of encountering and relating to a being opens the natural possibility of actions not following the script of the intended ritual, the most dramatic (and most visible in the archaeological record) being the deliberate damaging of images. After having attracted limited attention for a long time in Egyptology, the topic of 'iconoclasm' has become the focus of a number of recent studies (Wilson 2005; Bryan 2012; Ritner 2012; Connor 2018; Bleiberg and Weissberg 2019; Quack 2019; for Late Antique attacks on ancient Egyptian images, see also Myrup Kristensen 2013).

In past Egyptological research, there has been a tendency to conflate actual iconoclasm (damaging images as a goal in its own right) with different forms of reuse of monuments of the past, often designated with the reproving term 'usurpation' (e.g. Wilson 2005: 113–14, though problematized on pp. 130–1).

Reuse of monuments was, however – somewhat surprisingly to modern intuitions – an acceptable and often even respectful gesture in ancient Egypt, which comes to appear in a new light in the perspective on images taken here. As such, Egyptian practices of reuse are a prime example of what Bruno Latour (2002: 16) has labelled *iconoclash*, namely 'when one does not know, one hesitates, one is troubled by an action for which there is no way to know, without further enquiry, whether it is destructive or constructive'. For this reason, it is useful to examine the deliberate destruction of works of the past as a phenomenon separate from that of reuse.

One motivation for removing names and images of controversial past rulers was the well known one of *damnatio memoriae*, where such rulers as the female pharaoh Hatshepsut or the unsuccessful religious reformer Akhenaten were not only omitted from lists of past kings, but also had their monuments deliberately targeted to erase their memory (Bryan 2012).

More obscure is the widespread practice of targeted damaging of statues, in particular directed against the eyes and nose as well as either or both arms (Bleiberg and Weissberg 2019; Fig. 24). In many cases, it can be difficult to assess whether such damage is accidental or deliberate, but Egyptologist Edward Bleiberg has recently argued that such damages are so widespread and so specific that there can be little doubt as to the importance of the practice (ibid.). If Bleiberg's analysis is correct, the practice of breaking off noses and hands would be ways of deactivating the statue, though naturally the purposes for doing so can only be conjectured; in many cases, we are perhaps dealing with tomb robbers wanting to stymie the violated tomb owner's ability to take revenge (as tomb owners frequently threaten to do in their inscriptions). In the terminology espoused here, this would be a way of cancelling very specific affects of the image, notably the ability to presentify the depicted person, because the statue becomes unable to enter into the requisite relationships (such as receiving incense and other offerings, or in the case of worshipping statues, the ability to elicit the relation to the god). The relationship between such actions and conceptions of the body and its parts attestable through other sources (e.g. Nyord 2009) is a topic worthy of further investigation.

One particular episode of iconoclasm is worth discussing in a bit more detail, because it has, even quite recently, been taken to indicate a complete break with traditional Egyptian conceptions of images. As seen in Section 3.2, King Akhenaten apparently argued against the efficacy of traditional divine images, and the new solar cult he instated was characterized by a lack of anthropomorphic images of his new sun god, the Aten (Fig. 25). At the same time, he had images of the traditional sun god Amun-Re and his divine family removed from the monuments in and around Thebes.

Fig. 24 Kneeling statue of Yuny showing deliberate damage to the eyes and nose – favorite areas to attack in order to deactivate the presentifying function of an image. Metropolitan Museum of Art, 33.2.1.

In a recent book, Egyptologist James Hoffmeier (2015: 203) has argued that these acts of iconoclasm demonstrate that Akhenaten's religion was monotheist. Hoffmeier seems to have in mind the well-known historical acts of iconoclasm by Christians and Muslims against the images of other religions, but he does not lay out the exact premises of this conclusion. To conclude from the destruction of images to the existence of monotheist beliefs, however, seems to presuppose that the act of destroying an image can be seen as an expression to the effect that the god in question is not a true god. As seen, ancient Egyptian cultural history offers a number of examples of destruction of religious images, none of which seems to be motivated along these lines. On the other hand, Akhenaten and his followers are the only ancient Egyptians to whom monotheistic beliefs have been ascribed in the recent history of Egyptology, so that, if this idea is correct, it would in fact be justified to assume they had exceptional motivations. However, influential typologies of iconoclasm such as those of art historian David Freedberg (1989: 378–428) and sociologist Bruno Latour (2002) have shown the wide range of motivations that can lead to what is apparently one and the same action: that of damaging or destroying an image. We should thus examine the precise acts carried out by Akhenaten's followers to see if they might be motivated by more traditional Egyptian conceptions of images, or whether these acts do indeed demonstrate monotheistic beliefs.

While Hoffmeier cites some very occasional examples of destruction of the names of deities not directly connected with the Theban family of Amun at the temple of Amada in Nubia (Hoffmeier 2015: 199), it is probably more telling that a large number of monuments that were clearly visited by Akhenaten's people had names and depictions of other gods, which were left intact (Krauss 2000). This indicates that if there ever was a goal of erasing all other gods than the Aten, there were clear differences in priorities. This in itself speaks against a motivation of monotheistic fervour – if the acts were carried out because all other named and depicted gods were deemed unworthy of worship, it is unlikely that this would be true of some of the 'pagan' gods more than others.

An interesting additional pattern of destruction not mentioned by Hoffmeier is that of destroying images of a specific kind of priest, the so-called *s(t)m*-priest, highly recognizable by his ritual garb including a leopard/ cheetah skin (Bryan 2012: 375–6; Quack 2019: 56–7). While the precise reason for this is uncertain, at least it gives a strong indication that the destruction of names and images is more likely motivated by the cultic and ritual roles of the depicted entities than by a wish to eradicate all other gods than that of Akhenaten.

Given what has been said concerning Egyptian conceptions and experiences of images, it is inherently unlikely that images were erased in order to express a lack of belief in specific gods. Images were not generally seen as statements about the existence of the depicted entities. Similarly, the notion that a particular god is not a 'true' god or even does not exist would be difficult to reconcile with Egyptian ontology, occupied as it is with channelling and manifesting power. Gods always have a somewhat elusive existence, and it is the purpose of images and other objects and places to fix their existence (often temporarily) in time and space. As has been seen, then, the destruction of an image tends to be a negation of the presence, affects, and configuration embodied by the image, not a statement about the absolute existential status of the depicted.

Thus, the argument that Akhenaten revealed himself as a monotheist by destroying (certain) images of the traditional gods can be seen to be circular: The destruction of images is understood within a particular (monotheistic) framework as evidence of a negation of the existence of other gods, and this in turn is used to argue that the practice was motivated by monotheism in the first place. If we reject this approach as flawed, what can we say about Akhenaten's destruction of images, if we assume that he was reacting to

Fig. 25 Akhenaten making offerings to his god the Aten, manifested not in an image, but instead in the visible sun in the sky (with the sunrays as arms allowing interaction between the sky and the earth). Courtesy of the Penn Museum; image no. 175960, object no. E16230.

traditional ancient Egyptian conceptions of images? The destruction of images of the priest with leopard skin is instructive in this regard, as it shows that it was not other gods than the Aten that were targeted as such, but rather specific cultic forms which were regarded as problematic. This immediately brings us much closer to Egyptian conceptions of images as explored throughout this work in that it is the capacity of the image to configure and make present specific powers which most likely underlies Akhenaten's destruction of images. In this perspective, Amun and his family are not targeted because they were regarded as pagan idols, but rather because Akhenaten introduced new ways of actualizing the solar, royal, and ancestral powers that those traditional forms embodied. This also helps explain why the destruction seems to be focused particularly on monuments from the relatively recent past. We may assume that those monuments were still in use and that for this reason it became important to update the cultic forms – not necessarily for purely dogmatic reasons, but more likely for practical ritual ones.

To take up the second main motivation for making changes to artworks of the past, ancient Egypt offers countless examples of various types of reuse of earlier monuments (Brand 2010). Buildings were dismantled and used in foundations or as filling in the large entrance towers of Egyptian temples known as pylons (Björkman 1971), sometimes, but by no means always, related to other, clearly destructive acts of *damnatio memoriae* targeted at the builder (e.g. Akhenaten's buildings at Karnak, Vergnieux 1999). Blocks from old monuments were transported deliberately over significant distances to incorporate them in new ones (e.g. Goedicke 1971; Gilli 2009). On a smaller scale, ancient statuary was repurposed by removing the predecessor's name, possibly re-carving parts of the sculpture, and substituting one's own name instead (e.g. Magen 2011), and even coffins were quite frequently reworked to be used by new owners (e.g. Cooney 2017). While such practices were thus widespread and must to some extent have been deemed expectable or even acceptable, there are nonetheless countless injunctions in private tombs against damaging or reusing the materials of the tomb (e.g. Ritner 2012: 396–7; Bleiberg and Weissberg 2019: 31–2), perhaps revealing the anxiety that this might happen to one's own tomb while it was still (supposed to be) ritually active.

Art historian Dario Gamboni (1997) has suggested that the damaging or destruction of artworks can fruitfully be regarded as simply another episode of their ongoing creation, and, as already suggested, this seems a particularly useful approach to such practices of reuse. Traditional Western ideas such as the sanctity of works of art and the tomb as an inviolable site of eternal repose do not seem to have been experienced by the Egyptians in quite the same way.

The reuse of statuary underscores some of the features of Egyptian conceptions of images that we have already noted in other types of material. The practice of appropriating an image of someone else simply by adding a new name emphasizes once again that mimetic likeness is not a deciding criterion for establishing a relationship between depiction and depicted. Rather, taking over what was once the material presence of a (more often than not illustrious) royal predecessor becomes a way of taking over the affects of a king of the past as one's own. Nonetheless, it is clear that the need was sometimes seen to adjust those affects and the bodily form, sometimes perhaps to approach a mimetic compatibility (be it to the new point of reference or other images that the old image was to relate to), but also to rework other affects such as those embodied in crowns and other elements of iconography to render the image suitable for its new interactive context. Such adjustments may well have taken on a performative aspect by themselves, as in the case of no doubt very public displays of moving and reinstalling colossal statues of royal predecessors.

5 Conclusion

This Element has explored some central aspects of ancient Egyptian conceptions and experiences of images. The focus was deliberately put on the 'alterity' of Egyptian images – those features where the Egyptian understanding differs radically from ours, or where our only available vocabulary would relegate Egyptian practices to categories of 'magical' or otherwise 'irrational' behaviour. What has been left out of focus by this choice is a range of phenomena where we do find some overlap between ancient and modern image practices, such as narratives, symbolism and self-presentation (all of which have prominent sections among the papers in Hartwig 2015). While these topics have only been touched upon, however, it is likely that they may also appear in a new light when considered as instantiations of the image concepts explored here.

In many ways, the ideas and experiences discussed in this Element differ from the expectations a modern museum visitor may have of the Egyptian images he or she sees. We hope ancient images can bring us face to face with the long-dead people depicted, but if we expect to do so through naturalistic portraits, we may have the wrong idea. On the other hand, if we think along with Egyptian concepts of likeness, the images give us a deeper sense of the nature of the person depicted and the interactive context for which the image was made than any mere portrait could. If we see brute material masterfully bent to the sheer will of the artist, we are also unlikely to capture ancient experiences. Instead, we can train ourselves to see the depicted shapes as emerging from the material in which they were already present. In the same way, it is tempting to 'read' Egyptian images semiotically as mediums for communication, but we may come closer to Egyptian ideas by thinking of 'iconography' as calling forth the power instantiated by the image – simply to be present, as in amulets, or to enter more complex relationships with other material manifestations.

Ancient Egyptian conceptions and experiences of images thus run counter to representationalism in a number of different ways. This Element has attempted to develop a conceptual framework for capturing the different uses of images through a combination of analyses of the indigenous (emic) terminology and theoretical (etic) perspectives on such concepts as relationality and affect. The result is one where many of our intuitive distinctions turn out to be unhelpful, such as those between material and shape, or medium and contents. Instead, it was suggested from the outset that what at first sight seems like symbolic representation can instead be more fruitfully viewed within the 'analogistic' ontology of the ancient Egyptians, as being so many ways of eliciting ontological connections between different parts of the cosmos. This vocabulary and ways of thinking should provide a useful starting point for future analyses of ancient Egyptian images.

References

Alberti, Benjamin. 2012. 'Cut, pinch and pierce: Image as practice among the Early Formative La Candelaria, first millennium AD, Northwest Argentina', in Ing-Marie Back Danielsson, Fredrik Fahlander, and Ylva Sjöstrand (eds.), *Encountering imagery: Materialities, perceptions, relations* (Department of Archaeology and Classical Studies, Stockholm University: Stockholm).

2016. 'Archaeologies of ontology', *Annual Review of Archaeology*, 45: 163–79.

Andrews, Carol. 1994. *Amulets of ancient Egypt* (British Museum Press: London).

Angenot, Valérie, and Francesco Tiradritti (eds.). 2016. *Artists and colour in ancient Egypt: Proceedings of the colloquium held in Montepulciano, August 22nd–24th, 2008* (Missione Archeologica Italiana a Luxor: Montepulciano).

Assmann, Jan. 1969. *Liturgische Lieder an den Sonnengott* (Bruno Hessling: Munich).

1988. 'Ikonographie der Schönheit im alten Ägypten', in Theo Stemmler (ed.), *Schöne Frauen, schöne Männer: Literarische Schönheitsbeschreibungen. 2. Kolloquium der Forschungsstelle für europäische Literatur des Mittelalters* (Narr: Mannheim).

1992. 'Der Tempel der ägyptischen Spätzeit als Kanonisierung kultureller Identität', in Jürgen Osing and Erland Kolding Nielsen (eds.), *The heritage of ancient Egypt: Studies in honour of Erik Iversen* (Museum Tusculanum: Copenhagen).

2001 [1984]. *The search for god in ancient Egypt* (Cornell University Press: Ithaca and London).

2009. 'Altägyptische Bildpraxen und ihre impliziten Theorien', in Klaus Sachs-Hombach (ed.), *Bildtheorien: Anthropologische und kulturelle Grundlagen des Visualistic Turn* (Suhrkamp: Frankfurt).

2015. 'Le pouvoir des images: De la performativité des images en Égypte ancienne', in Emmanuel Alloa (ed.), *Penser l'image II: Anthropologies du visuel* (Les presses du réel: Paris).

Aufrère, Sydney. 1991. *L'univers minéral dans la pensée égyptienne* (Institut Français d'Archéologie Orientale: Cairo).

Bahrani, Zainab. 2003. *The graven image: Representation in Babylonia and Assyria* (University of Pennsylvania Press: Philadelphia).

2014. *The infinite image: Art, time and the aesthetic dimension in antiquity* (Reaktion Books: London).

Baines, John. 1985. *Fecundity figures: Egyptian personification and the iconology of a genre* (Aris & Phillips: Warminster).

1990. 'Restricted knowledge, hierarchy, and decorum: Modern perceptions and ancient institutions', *Journal of the American Research Center in Egypt*, 27: 1–23.

2007. *Visual and written culture in ancient Egypt* (Oxford University Press: Oxford and New York).

2015. 'What is art?', in Melinda Hartwig (ed.), *A companion to ancient Egyptian art* (Wiley Blackwell: Chichester).

Barad, Karen. 2007. *Meeting the universe halfway: Quantum physics and the entanglement of matter and meaning* (Duke University Press: Durham and London).

Barns, John W. B. 1956. *Five Ramesseum Papyri* (Griffith Institute: Oxford).

Bechler, Zev. 1995. *Aristotle's theory of actuality* (State University of New York Press: Albany).

Belting, Hans. 1994. *Likeness and presence: A history of the image before the era of art* (University of Chicago Press: Chicago).

2016. 'Iconic presence: Images in religious traditions', *Material Religion*, 12: 235–37.

Bennett, Jane. 2010. *Vibrant matter: A political ecology of things* (Duke University Press: Durham and London).

Berlev, Oleg. 2003. 'Two kings – two suns: On the worldview of the ancient Egyptians', in Stephen Quirke (ed.), *Discovering Egypt from the Neva: The Egyptological legacy of Oleg D. Berlev* (Achet Verlag: Berlin).

Bestock, Laurel. 2018. *Violence and power in ancient Egypt: Image and ideology before the New Kingdom* (Routledge: Abingdon and New York).

Björkman, Gun. 1971. *Kings at Karnak: A study of the treatment of the monuments of royal predecessors in the early New Kingdom* (Uppsala University: Uppsala).

Bleiberg, Edward, and Stephanie Weissberg. 2019. *Striking power: Iconoclasm in ancient Egypt* (Brooklyn Museum and Pulitzer Arts Foundation: Brooklyn and St. Louis).

Blumenthal, Elke. 1970. *Untersuchungen zum ägyptischen Königtum des Mittleren Reiches* (Akademie-Verlag: Berlin).

Bolt, Barbara. 2004. *Art beyond representation: The performative power of the image* (I.B. Tauris: London and New York).

Borchardt, Ludwig. 1934. *Statuen und Statuetten von Königen und Privatleuten IV* (Reichsdruckerei: Berlin).

Borghouts, Joris F. 1971. *The magical texts of Papyrus Leiden I 348* (Brill: Leiden).

1982. 'Divine intervention in ancient Egypt and its manifestation', in R. J. Demarée and Jac J. Janssen (eds.), *Gleanings from Deir el-Medîna* (Nederlands Instituut voor het Nabije Oosten: Leiden).

2008. 'Trickster gods in the Egyptian pantheon', in Stephen E. Thompson and Peter Der Manuelian (eds.), *Egypt and beyond: Essays presented to Leonard H. Lesko upon his retirement from the Wilbour Chair of Egyptology at Brown University June 2005* (Brown University, Department of Egyptology and Ancient Western Asian Studies: Providence).

Boyer, Pascal. 1994. *Tradition as truth and communication: A cognitive description of traditional discourses* (Cambridge University Press: Cambridge).

Brand, Peter. 2010. 'Reuse and restoration', in Willeke Wendrich (ed.), *UCLA Encyclopedia of Egyptology* (eScholarship: Los Angeles).

Braun, Nadja S. 2009. 'The ancient Egyptian conception of images', *Lund Archaeological Review*, 15: 103–14.

Brémont, Axelle. 2018. 'Into the wild? Rethinking the Dynastic conception of the desert beyond nature and culture', *Journal of Ancient Egyptian Interconnections*, 17: 1–17.

Brown, Peter. 1981. *The cult of the saints: Its rise and function in Latin Christianity* (University of Chicago Press: Chicago and London).

Brunner, Hellmut. 1986. *Die Geburt des Gottkönigs: Studien zur Überlieferung eines altägyptischen Mythos* (Harrasowitz: Wiesbaden).

Bryan, Betsy M. 2012. 'Episodes of iconoclasm in the Egyptian New Kingdom', in Natalie Naomi May (ed.), *Iconoclasm and text destruction in the ancient Near East and beyond* (Oriental Institute: Chicago).

2017a. 'The ABC of painting in the mid-Eighteenth Dynasty: Terminology and social meaning', in Robert K. Ritner (ed.), *Essays for the Library of Seshat: Studies Presented to Janet H. Johnson on the occasion of her 70th birthday* (The Oriental Institute of the University of Chicago: Chicago).

2017b. 'Art-making in text and context', in Richard Jasnow and Ghislaine Widmer (eds.), *Illuminating Osiris: Egyptological studies in honor of Mark Smith* (Lockwood Press: Atlanta).

Campagno, Marcello. 2014. 'Patronage and other logics of social organization in ancient Egypt during the IIIrd millennium BCE', *Journal of Egyptian History*, 7: 1–33.

Caritoux, Laurent. 2008. 'Du bûcheron au menusier: Comment un meuble devient *mnḫ*', *Égypte, Afrique & Orient*, 49: 17 56.

Černý, Jaroslav. 1939. *Catalogue des ostraca hiératiques non littéraires de Deir El Médineh*, vol. IV (Institut Français d'Archéologie Orientale: Cairo).

Chauvet, Violaine. 2015. 'Who did what and why? The dynamics of tomb preparation', in Richard Jasnow and Kathlyn M. Cooney (eds.), *Joyful in Thebes: Egyptological studies in honor of Betsy M. Bryan* (Lockwood Press: Atlanta).

Connor, Simon. 2016–2017. 'Pierres et statues: Représentation du roi et des particuliers sous Sésostris III', *Cahiers de Recherces de l'Institut de Papyrologie et d'Égyptologie de Lille*, 31: 5–28.

2018. 'Mutiler, tuer, désactiver les images en Égypte pharaonique', *Perspective: Actualité en histoire d'art*, 2018: 147–66.

Cooney, Kathlyn M. 2007. *The cost of death: The social and economic value of ancient Egyptian funerary art in the Ramesside Period* (Nederlands Instituut voor het Nabije Oosten: Leiden).

2017. 'Coffin reuse: Ritual materialism in the context of scarcity', in Alessia Amenta and Hélène Guichard (eds.), *Proceedings First Vatican Coffin Conference, 19–22 June 2013* (Edizioni Musei Vaticani: Vatican City).

Couyat, J., and P. Montet. 1912. *Les inscriptions hiéroglyphiques et hiératiques du Ouâdi Hammâmât* (Institut Français d'Archéologique Orientale: Cairo).

Cruz-Uribe, Eugene. 1999. 'Opening of the mouth as temple ritual', in Emily Teeter and John A. Larson (eds.), *Gold of praise: Studies on ancient Egypt in honor of Edward F. Wente* (Oriental Institute: Chicago).

d'Azevedo, Warren L. (ed.). 1989 [1973]. *The traditional artist in African societies* (Indiana University Press: Bloomington and Indianapolis).

Daninos, Albert. 1886. 'Lettre de M. Daninos-Bey à M. G. Maspero, directeur général des fouilles et musées d'Égypte au sujet de la découverte des statues de Meidoum', *Recueil de Travaux relatifs à la philologie et à l'archéologie égyptiennes et assyriennes*, 8: 69–73.

Darnell, John Coleman, and Colleen Manassa Darnell. 2018. *The ancient Egyptian netherworld books* (SBL Press: Atlanta).

David, Rosalie. 2018. *Temple ritual at Abydos* (Egypt Exploration Society: London).

Davies, N. de Garis. 1920. *The tomb of Antefoker, vizier of Sesostris I, and of his wife, Senet (No. 60)* (George Allen & Unwin: London).

Den Doncker, Alexis. 2010. 'Prélude à une étude de la réception de l'image égyptienne par les anciens Égyptiens', in Eugène Warmenbol and Valérie Angenot (eds.), *Thèbes aux 101 portes: Mélanges à la mémoire de Roland Tefnin* (Brepols: Turnhout).

Descola, Philippe (ed.). 2010. *La fabrique des images: Visions du monde et formes de la représentation* (Musée du Quai Branly and Somogy: Éditions d'art: Paris).

2013 [2005]. *Beyond nature and culture* (University of Chicago Press: Chicago and London).

Desroches-Noblecourt, Christiane. 1995. *Amours et fureurs de La Lointaine: Clés pour la compréhension de symboles égyptiens* (Stock-Pernoud: Paris).

2003. *Lorsque la nature parlait aux Égyptiens: Mythes et symboles au temps des pharaons* (Philippe Rey: Paris).

Dubiel, Ulrike. 2008. *Amulette, Siegel und Perlen: Studien zur Typologie und Tragesitte im Alten und Mittleren Reich* (Academic Press and Vandenhoeck & Ruprecht: Fribourg and Göttingen).

Eaton, Katherine. 2007. 'Types of cult-image carried in divine barques and the logistics of performing temple ritual in the New Kingdom', *Zeitschrift für Ägyptische Sprache und Altertumskunde*, 134: 15–25.

Eicke, Sven. 2017. 'Affecting the gods: Fear in ancient Egyptian religious texts', in Anne Storch (ed.), *Consensus and dissent: Negotiating emotion in the public space* (John Benjamins: Amsterdam and Philadelphia).

el-Shahawy, Abeer. 2005. *The Egyptian Museum in Cairo: A walk through the alleys of ancient Egypt* (Farid Atiya Press: Cairo).

Elkins, James. 2008. 'Can we invent a world art studies?', in Kitty Zijlmans and Wilfried van Damme (eds.), *World art studies: Exploring concepts and approaches* (Valiz: Amsterdam).

Emerit, Sibylle. 2011. 'Listening to the gods: Echoes of the divine in ancient Egypt', in Erika Meyer-Dietrich (ed.), *Laut und Leise: Der Gebrauch von Stimme und Klang in historischen Kulturen* (Transcript Verlag: Bielefeld).

Eschenbrenner-Diemer, Gersande. 2017. 'From the workshop to the grave: The case of wooden funerary models', in Gianluca Miniaci, Marilina Betrò and Stephen Quirke (eds.), *Company of images: Modelling the imaginary world of Middle Kingdom Egypt (2000–1550 BC) – Proceedings of the international conference of the EPOCHS Project held 18th–20th September 2014 at UCL, London* (Peeters: Leuven, Paris, and Bristol, CT).

Eschweiler, Peter. 1994. *Bildzauber im alten Ägypten: Die Verwendung von Bildern und Gegenständen in magischen Handlungen nach den Texten des Mittleren und Neuen Reiches* (Universitätsverlag and Vandenhoeck & Ruprecht: Freiburg and Göttingen).

Espirito Santo, Diana, and Nico Tassi. 2013. 'Introduction', in Diana Espirito Santo and Nico Tassi (eds.), *Making spirits: Materiality and transcendence in contemporary religions* (I.B. Tauris: London and New York).

Finnestad, Ragnhild Bjerre. 1989. 'Egyptian thought about life as a problem of translation', in Gertie Englund (ed.), *The religion of the ancient Egyptian: Cognitive structures and popular expressions – Proceedings of symposia in Uppsala and Bergen 1987 and 1988* (Uppsala University: Uppsala).

Fischer-Elfert, Hans-Werner. 1998. *Die Vision von der Statue im Stein: Studien zum altägyptischen Mundöffnungsritual* (Universitätsverlag C. Winter: Heidelberg).

Fitzenreiter, Martin. 2001. *Statue und Kult: Eine Studie der funerären Praxis an nichtköniglichen Grabanlagen der Residenz im Alten Reich* (Humboldt-Universität zu Berlin: Berlin).

2011. 'Wappenpflanzen', in Christian Tietze (ed.), *Ägyptische Gärten* (Arcus-Verlag: Weimar).

2019. 'Schon wieder Stele Louvre C 14 des Irtisen', *Göttinger Miszellen*, 257: 49–62.

Frandsen, Paul John. 1992. 'On the root *nfr* and a "clever" remark on embalming', in Jürgen Osing and Erland Kolding Nielsen (eds.), *The heritage of ancient Egypt: Studies in honour of Erik Iversen* (Museum Tusculanum Press: Copenhagen).

Freedberg, David. 1989. *The power of images: Studies in the history and theory of response* (University of Chicago Press: Chicago and London).

Frood, Elizabeth. 2019. 'When statues speak about themselves', in Aurélia Masson-Berghoff (ed.), *Statues in context: Production, meaning and (re)uses* (Peeters: Leuven).

Gadamer, Hans-Georg. 2004 [1960]. *Truth and method* (Continuum: London and New York).

Gamboni, Dario. 1997. *The destruction of art: Iconoclasm and vandalism since the French Revolution* (Reaktion Books: London).

Gardiner, Alan H. 1911. *Egyptian Hieratic Texts. Series I: Literary texts of the New Kingdom. Part I: The Papyrus Anastasi and the Papyrus Koller, together with parallel texts* (J.C. Hinrichs'sche Buchhandlung: Leipzig).

1937. *Late-Egyptian Miscellanies* (Fondation Égyptologique Reine Élisabeth: Brussels).

Gayet, Albert-J. 1889. *Musée du Louvre, stèles de la XIIe dynastie* (F. Vieweg: Paris).

Geimer, Peter. 2007. 'Gegensichtbarkeiten', *Bildwelten des Wissens: Kunsthistorisches Jahrbuch für Bildkritik*, 4: 33–42.

Gell, Alfred. 1992. 'The technology of enchantment and the enchantment of technology', in Jeremy Coote and Anthony Shelton (eds.), *Anthropology, art and aesthetics* (Oxford University Press: Oxford).

1998. *Art and agency: An anthropological theory* (Oxford University Press: Oxford).

Gibson, James J. 1966. *The senses considered as perceptual systems* (Houghton Mifflin: Boston).

Gillen, Todd (ed.). 2017. *(Re)productive traditions in ancient Egypt: Proceedings of the conference held at the University of Liège, 6th–8th February 2013* (Presses Universitaires de Liège: Liège).

Gilli, Barbara. 2009. 'The past in the present: The reuse of ancient material in the 12th Dynasty', *Aegyptus*: 89–110.

Goebs, Katja. 2011. 'King as god and god as king: Colour, light, and transformation in Egyptian ritual', in Rolf Gundlach and Kate Spence (eds.), *Palace and Temple: Architecture – Decoration – Ritual: Cambridge, July, 16th–17th, 2007* (Harrasowitz: Wiesbaden).

Goedicke, Hans. 1971. *Re-used blocks from the pyramid of Amenemhet I at Lisht* (Metropolitan Museum of Art: New York).

Gosden, Chris. 2001. 'Making sense: Archaeology and aesthetics', *World Archaeology*, 33: 163–7.

Goyon, Jean-Claude. 1972. *Rituels funéraires de l'ancienne Égypte: Le Rituel de l'ouverture de la bouche, les Livres des respirations* (Éditions du Cerf: Paris).

Grajetzki, Wolfram. 2003. *Burial customs in ancient Egypt: Life in death for rich and poor* (Duckworth: London).

Graves-Brown, Carolyn. 2006. 'Emergent flints', in Kasia Szpakowska (ed.), *Through a glass darkly: Magic, dreams and prophecy in ancient Egypt* (Classical Press of Wales: Swansea).

2010. 'The ideological significance of flint in dynastic Egypt', PhD thesis, University College London.

Haring, Ben J. J. 1997. *Divine households: Administrative and economic aspects of the New Kingdom royal memorial temples in western Thebes* (Nederlands Instituut voor het Nabije Oosten: Leiden).

Harman, Graham. 2018. *Object-Oriented Ontology: A new theory of everything* (Penguin: London).

Harris, Oliver. 2017a. 'Assemblages and scale in archaeology', *Cambridge Archaeological Journal*, 27: 127–39.

2017b. 'From emotional geographies to assemblages of affect: Emotion in archaeology in the light of the ontological turn', *Cologne Contributions to Archaeology and Cultural Studies*, 2: 93–112.

Harrison-Buck, Eleanor, and Julia A. Hendon (eds.). 2018. *Relational identities and other-than-human agency in archaeology* (University of Colorado Press: Boulder).

Hartwig, Melinda. 2004. *Tomb painting and identity in ancient Thebes, 1419–1372 BCE* (Brepols: Brussels).

(ed.). 2015. *A companion to ancient Egyptian art* (Wiley Blackwell: Chichester).

Hayes, William C. 1935. 'The tomb of Nefer-Khewet and his family', *Bulletin of the Metropolitan Museum of Art*, 30: 17–36.

Henare, Amiria, Martin Holbraad, and Sari Wastell. 2007. 'Introduction: Thinking through things', in Amiria Henare, Martin Holbraad and Sari Wastell (eds.), *Thinking through things: Theorising artefacts ethnographically* (Routledge: London and New York).

Hoffmann, Friedhelm. 2001. 'Wort und Bild: Texte und Untersuchungen zur ägyptischen Statuenbeschreibung', PhD thesis, University of Würzburg.

Hoffmann, Nadette. 1996. 'Reading the Amduat', *Zeitschrift für Ägyptische Sprache und Altertumskunde*, 123: 26–40.

Hoffmeier, James Karl. 2015. *Akhenaten and the origins of monotheism* (Oxford University Press: Oxford and New York).

Hornung, Erik. 1963. *Das Amduat: Die Schrift des verborgenen Raumes* (Harrasowitz: Wiesbaden).

1999. *The ancient Egyptian books of the afterlife* (Cornell University Press: Ithaca and London).

Ilin-Tomich, Alexander. 2017. *From workshop to sanctuary: The production of late Middle Kingdom memorial stelae* (Golden House Publications: London).

Ingold, Tim. 2013. *Making: Anthropology, archaeology, art and architecture* (Routledge: London and New York).

Jansen-Winkeln, Karl. 2014. *Inschriften der Spätzeit, Teil IV: Die 26. Dynastie* (Harrasowitz: Wiesbaden).

Janssen, Jac J. 1975. *Commodity prices from the Ramesside period: An economic study of the village of necroplis workmen at Thebes* (E.J. Brill: Leiden).

Jørgensen, Mogens. 2015. 'The quest for immortality: Reflections on some Egyptian "portraits" in the Ny Carlsberg Glyptotek', in Rune Nyord and Kim Ryholt (eds.), *Lotus and laurel: Studies on Egyptian language and religion in honour of Paul John Frandsen* (Museum Tusculanum: Copenhagen).

Junge, Friedrich. 1990. 'Versuch zu einer Ästhetik der ägyptischen Kunst', in Marianne Eaton-Krauss and Erhart Graefe (eds.), *Studien zur altägyptischen Kunstgeschichte* (Gerstenberg: Hildesheim).

Kanawati, Naguib. 2001. *The tomb and beyond: Burial customs of Egyptian officials* (Aris & Phillips: Warminster).

Keimer, Louis. 1940. 'Jeux de la nature retouchés par la main de l'homme, provenant de Deir el-Médineh (Thèbes) et remontant au Nouvel-Empire', *Études d'Égyptologie*, 2: 1–21.

Kjølby, Annette. 2009. 'Material agency, attribution and experience of agency in ancient Egypt: The case of New Kingdom private temple statues', in Rune Nyord and Annette Kjølby (eds.), *'Being in ancient Egypt: Thoughts on agency, materiality and cognition: Proceedings of the seminar held in Copenhagen, September 29–30 2006* (Archaeopress: Oxford).

Kozloff, Arielle P., Betsy M. Bryan, and Lawrence M. Berman. 1992. *Egypt's dazzling sun: Amenhotep III and his world* (Cleveland Museum of Art: Cleveland).

Krauss, Rolf. 2000. 'Akhenaten: Monotheist? Polytheist?', *Bulletin of the Australian Centre for Egyptology*, 11: 93–101.

Krönig, Wolfgang 1934. 'Ägyptische Faience-Schalen des Neuen Reiches. Eine motivgeschichtliche Untersuchung', *Mitteilungen des Deutschen Instituts für Ägyptische Altertumskunde in Kairo*, 5: 144–66.

Kuhlmann, Klaus P. 1973. 'Eine Beschreibung der Grabdekoration mit der Aufforderung zu kopieren und zum Hinterlassen von Besucherinschriften aus saitischer Zeit', *Mitteilungen des Deutschen Archäologischen Instituts, Abteilung Kairo*, 29: 205–13.

Kurth, Dieter. 1998. *Treffpunkt der Götter: Inschriften aus dem Tempel des Horus von Edfu* (Artemis & Winkler: Düsseldorf).

Laboury, Dimitri. 2010. 'Portrait versus ideal image', in Willeke Wendrich (ed.), *UCLA Encyclopedia of Egyptology* (eScholarship.org: Los Angeles).

———— 2013. 'L'artiste égyptien, ce grand méconnu de l'égyptologie', in Guillemette Andreu-Lanoë (ed.), *L'art du contour: Le dessin dans l'Égypte ancienne* (Louvre éditions: Paris).

———— 2017. 'Tradition and creativity: Toward a study of intericonicity in ancient Egyptian art', in Todd Gillen (ed.), *(Re)productive traditions in ancient Egypt: Proceedings of the conference held at the University of Liège, 6th-8th February 2013* (Presses universitaires de Liège: Liège).

Lallemand, Henri. 1922. 'Les assemblages dans la technique égyptienne et le sens originel du mot menkh', *Bulletin de l'Institut Français d'Archéologie Orientale*, 22: 77–98.

Lange, Hans O., and Heinrich Schäfer. 1902. *Grab- und Denksteine des Mittleren Reichs im Museum von Kairo, No. 20001–20780* (Reichsdruckerei: Berlin).

Lapp, Günther. 1997. *The papyrus of Nu* (British Museum Press: London).

Latour, Bruno. 2002. 'What is iconoclash? Or is there a world beyond the image wars?', in Peter Weibel and Bruno Latour (eds.), *Iconoclash: Beyond the image-wars in science, religion and art* (MIT Press: Cambridge, MA and London).

2009. 'Perspectivism: "Type" or "bomb"?', *Anthropology Today*, 25: 1–2.

Lehmann, Katja. 2000. 'Der Serdab in den Privatgräbern des Alten Reiches', PhD thesis, Universität Heidelberg.

Lekov, Teodor. 2005. 'Ancient Egyptian notion of *ka* according to the Pyramid Texts', *Journal of Egyptological Studies*, 2: 11–37.

Lieven, Alexandra von. 2007. 'Im Schatten des Goldhauses: Berufsgeheimnis und Handwerkerinitation im Alten Ägypten', *Studien zur Altägyptischen Kultur*, 36: 147–56.

Lorton, David. 1999. 'The theology of cult statues in ancient Egypt', in Michael Brennan Dick (ed.), *Born in heaven, made on earth: The making of the cult image in the ancient Near East* (Eisenbrauns: Winona Lake).

Lüscher, Barbara. 1998. *Untersuchungen zu Totenbuch Spruch 151* (Harrasowitz: Wiesbaden).

Magen, Barbara. 2011. *Steinerne Palimpseste: Zur Wiederverwendung von Statuen durch Ramses II und seine Nachfolger* (Harrasowitz: Wiesbaden).

Manassa, Colleen. 2011. 'Soundscapes in ancient Egyptian literature and religion', in Erika Meyer-Dietrich (ed.), *Laut und Leise: Der Gebrauch von Stimme und Klang in historischen Kulturen* (Transcript Verlag: Bielefeld).

Mathieu, Bernard. 2016. 'Irtysen le technicien (stèle Louvre C 14)', in Valérie Angenot and Francesco Tiradritti (eds.), *Artists and colour in ancient Egypt: Proceedings of the colloquium held in Montepulciano, August 22nd–24th, 2008* (Missione Archeologica Italiana a Luxor: Montepulciano).

Matić, Uroš. 2018. 'The sap of life: Materiality and sex in the divine birth legend of Hatshepsut and Amenhotep III', in Érika Maynart, Carolina Velloza and Rennan Lemos (eds.), *Perspectives on materiality in ancient Egypt: Agency, cultural reproduction and change* (Archaeopress: Oxford).

McDowell, Angela. 2002. *Village life in ancient Egypt: Laundry lists and love songs* (Oxford University Press: Oxford and New York).

Meskell, Lynn. 2002. *Private life in New Kingdom Egypt* (Princeton University Press: Princeton).

2004. *Object worlds in ancient Egypt: Material biographies past and present* (Berg: Oxford and New York).

Milward, A. J. 1982. 'Bowls', in Rita E. Freed (ed.), *Egypt's Golden Age: The Art of Living in the New Kingdom, 1558–1085 B.C.* (Museum of Fine Arts: Boston).

Miniaci, Gianluca. 2018. 'Faience craftsmanship in the Middle Kingdom: A market paradox: inexpensive materials for prestige goods', in Gianluca Miniaci, Juan Carlos Moreno García, Stephen Quirke, and Andréas Stauder (eds.), *The arts of making in ancient Egypt: Voices, images, and object of material producers 2000–1550 BCE* (Sidestone Press: Leiden).

Miniaci, Gianluca, Juan Carlos Moreno García, Stephen Quirke, and Andréas Stauder (eds.). 2018. *The arts of making in ancient Egypt. Voices, images, and object of material producers 2000–1550 BCE* (Sidestone Press: Leiden).

Mitchell, W. J. T. 2005. *What do pictures really want? The lives and loves of images* (University of Chicago Press: Chicago).

Moje, Jan. 2006. 'O.DeM 246: Ein Auftragsbeleg aus einer altägyptischen Werkstatt', *Bulletin de l'Institut Français d'Archéologie Orientale*, 106: 183–92.

Morenz, Siegfried. 1964. *Die Herauskunft des transzendenten Gottes in Ägypten* (Akademie-Verlag: Berlin).

Morphy, Howard. 1989. 'From dull to brilliant: The aesthetics of spiritual power among the Yolngu', *Man N.S.*, 24: 21–40.

Müller, Maya. 1990. 'Die ägyptische Kunst aus kunsthistorischer Sicht', in Marianne Eaton-Krauss and Erhart Graefe (eds.), *Studien zur ägyptischen Kunstgeschichte* (Gerstenberg: Hildesheim).

1998. 'Egyptian aesthetics in the Middle Kingdom', in Chris Eyre (ed.), *Proceedings of the Seventh International Congress of Egyptologists, Cambridge 3–9 September 1995* (Peeters: Leuven).

2003. 'Die Göttin im Boot: Eine ikonographische Untersuchung', in Tobias Hofmann and Alexandra Sturm (eds.), *Menschenbilder – Bildermenschen: Kunst und Kultur im alten Ägypten* (Books on Demand: Norderstedt).

2006. 'Die Königsplastik des Mittleren Reiches und ihre Schöpfer: Reden über Statuen – Wenn Statuen reden', *Imago Aegypti*, 1: 27–78.

2012. 'Discourses about art in ancient and modern times', in Katalin Anna Kóthay (ed.), *Art and society: Ancient and modern contexts of Egyptian art – Proceedings of the international conference held at the Museum of Fine Arts, Budapest, 13–15 May 2010* (Museum of Fine Arts: Budapest).

Kristensen, Troels Myrup. 2013. *Making and breaking the gods: Christian responses to pagan sculpture in Late Antiquity* (Aarhus University Press: Aarhus).

Needham, Rodney. 1972. *Belief, language, experience* (University of Chicago Press: Chicago).

Neer, Richard. 2017. 'Was the Knidia a statue? Art history and the terms of comparison', in Jaś Elsner (ed.), *Comparativism in art history* (Routledge: London and New York).

Newberry, Percy E. 1893. *Beni Hasan*, Part I (Kegan Paul, Trench, Trübner & Co: London).

Nicholson, Paul. 1998. 'Materials and technology', in Florence D. Friedman (ed.), *Gifts of the Nile: Ancient Egyptian faience* (Thames and Hudson: London and New York).

Nyord, Rune. 2009. *Breathing flesh: Conceptions of the body in the ancient Egyptian Coffin Texts* (Museum Tusculanum Press: Copenhagen).

2013a. 'Memory and succession in the city of the dead: Temporality in the ancient Egyptian mortuary cult', in Dorthe Refslund Christensen and Rane Willerslev (eds.), *Taming time, timing death* (Ashgate: Farnham).

2013b. 'Vision and conceptualization in ancient Egyptian art', in Rosario Caballero and Javier E. Díaz Vera (eds.), *Sensuous cognition: Explorations into human sentience: Imagination, (e)motion and perception* (De Gruyter: Berlin).

2014. 'Permeable containers. Body and cosmos in Middle Kingdom coffins', in Rogério Sousa (ed.), *Body, cosmos and eternity: New research trends in the iconography and symbolism of ancient Egyptian coffins* (Archaeopress: Oxford).

2017. '"An image of the owner as he was on earth": Representation and ontology in Middle Kingdom funerary images', in Gianluca Miniaci, Marilina Betrò, and Stephen Quirke (eds.), *Company of images: Modelling the imaginary world of Middle Kingdom Egypt (2000–1550 BC) – Proceedings of the international conference of the EPOCHS Project held 18th–20th September 2014 at UCL, London* (Peeters: Leuven, Paris, and Bristol, CT).

2018a. 'Death before time: Mythical time in ancient Egyptian mortuary religion', in Sophie Seebach and Rane Willerslev (eds.), *Mirrors of passing: Unlocking the mysteries of death, materiality, and time* (Berghahn: New York and Oxford).

2018b. '"Taking ancient Egyptian mortuary religion seriously": Why would we, and how could we?', *Journal of Ancient Egyptian Interconnections*, 17: 73–87.

2019. 'The concept of *ka* between Egyptian and Egyptological frameworks', in Rune Nyord (ed.), *Concepts in Middle Kingdom funerary culture: Proceedings of the Lady Wallis Budge Anniversary Sympoisum held at Christ's College, Cambridge, 22 January 2016* (Brill: Leiden and Boston).

2020. 'The Nile in the hippopotamus: Being and becoming in faience figurines of Middle Kingdom ancient Egypt', in Ing-Marie Back Danielsson and Andrew Jones (eds.), *Images in the making: Art, process, archaeology* (Manchester University Press: Manchester).

Ockinga, Boyo. 1984. *Die Gottebenbildlichkeit im alten Ägypten und im Alten Testament* (Harrasowitz: Wiesbaden).

Osing, Jürgen. 1976. 'Ächtungstexte aus dem Alten Reich (II)', *Mitteilungen des Deutschen Archäologischen Instituts, Abteilung Kairo*, 32: 133–85.

Pellini, José Roberto. 2018. *Senses, affects and archaeology: Changing the heart, the mind and the pants* (Cambridge Scholars Publishing: Newcastle).

Pieper, Max. 1929. *Die grosse Inschrift des Königs Neferhotep in Abydos* (J. C. Hinrichs: Leipzig).

Pinch, Geraldine. 1993. *Votive offerings to Hathor* (Griffith Institute: Oxford).

Pommerening, Tanja, Elena Marinova, and Stan Hendrickx. 2010. 'The Early Dynastic origin of the water-lily motif', *Chronique d'Égypte*, 85: 14–40.

Price, Campbell. 2016. 'On the function of "healing" statues', in Campbell Price, Roger Forshaw, Andrew Chamberlain, Paul T. Nicholson, and Robert Morkot (eds.), *Mummies, magic and medicine in ancient Egypt: Multidisciplinary essays for Rosalie David* (Manchester University Press: Manchester).

2017. '"His image as perfect as the ancestors": On the transmission of forms in non-royal sculpture during the First Millennium B.C.', in Todd Gillen (ed.), *(Re)productive traditions in ancient Egypt: Proceedings of the conference held at the University of Liège, 6th–8th February 2013* (Presses Universitaires de Liège: Liège).

Price, Robyn. 2018. 'Sniffing out the gods: Archaeology with the senses', *Journal of Ancient Egyptian Interconnections*, 17: 137–55.

Putter, Thierry De. 1997. 'Ramsès II, géologue? Un commentaire de la stèle de Manshiyet es-Sadr, dite "de l'an 8"', *Zeitschift für Ägyptische Sprache und Altertumskunde*, 124: 131–41.

Quack, Joachim Friedrich. 2002. 'Some Old Kingdom execration figurines from the Teti cemetery', *Bulletin of the Australian Centre for Egyptology*, 13: 149–60.

2018. 'Incense, the alphabet and other elements', in Nikolas Jaspert and Sebastian Kolditz (eds.), *Entre mers – Outre-mer: Spaces, modes and agents of Indo-Mediterranean connectivity* (Heidelberg University Publishing: Heidelberg).

2019. '"Lösche seinen Namen aus!" Zur Vernichtung von personenreferen-zierter Schrift und Bild im Alten Ägypten', in Carina Kühne-Wespi, Klaus Peter Oschema and Joachim Friedrich Quack (eds.), *Zerstörung von Geschriebenem: Historische und transkulturelle Perspektiven* (De Gruyter: Berlin and Boston).

Quirke, Stephen. 1986. 'The hieratic texts in the tomb of Nakht the gardener', *Journal of Egyptian Archaeology*, 72: 79–90.

2003. '"Art" and "the artist" in late Middle Kingdom administration', in Stephen Quirke (ed.), *Discovering Egypt from the Neva: The Egyptological legacy of Oleg D Berlev* (Achet Verlag: Berlin).

2013. *Going out in daylight – prt m hrw: The ancient Egyptian Book of the Dead – translation, sources, meanings* (Golden House Publications: London).

2015. *Exploring religion in ancient Egypt* (Wiley Blackwell: Chichester).

Raven, Maarten J. 1988. 'Magic and symbolic aspects of certain materials in ancient Egypt', *Varia Aegyptiaca*, 4: 237–42.

Redford, Donald B. 1981. 'A royal speech from the blocks of the 10th pylon', *Bulletin of the Egyptological Seminar*, 3: 87–102.

Reeves, Nicholas. 2001. *Ancient Egypt: The great discoveries* (Thames and Hudson: London and New York).

Régen, Isabelle. 2010. 'When the Book of the Dead does not match archaeology: The case of the protective magical bricks (BD 151)', *British Museum Studies in Ancient Egypt and Sudan*, 15: 267–78.

Riggs, Christina. 2014. *Unwrapping ancient Egypt* (Bloomsbury Academic: London and New York).

2017. 'In the shadows: The study of ancient Egyptian art', *Orientalistische Literaturzeitung*, 112: 293–300.

Ritner, Robert K. 1993. *The mechanics of ancient Egyptian magical practice* (Oriental Institute of the University of Chicago: Chicago).

2012. 'Killing the image, killing the essence: The destruction of text and figures in ancient Egyptian thought, ritual, and "ritualized history"', in Natalie Naomi May (ed.), *Iconoclasm and text destruction in the ancient Near East and beyond* (Oriental Institute: Chicago).

Robb, John. 2015. 'What do things want? Object design as a middle range theory of material culture', *Archeological Papers of the American Anthropological Association*, 26: 166–80.

Robins, Gay. 1994. *Proportion and style in ancient Egyptian art* (Thames and Hudson: London).

1998. 'Piles of offerings: Paradigms of limitation and creativity in ancient Egyptian art', in Christopher J. Eyre (ed.), *Proceedings of the Seventh International Congress of Egyptologists, Cambridge, 3–9 September 1995* (Peeters: Leuven).

2008. *The art of ancient Egypt* (British Museum Press: London).

Roccati, Alessandro. 2011. *Magia Taurinensia: Il grande papiro magico di Torino e i suoi duplicati* (Gregorian & Biblical Press: Rome).

Rummel, Ute. 2016. 'Der Leib der Göttin: Materialität und Semantik ägyptischer Felslandschaft', in Susanne Beck, Burkhard Backes, I-Ting Liao, Henrike Simon and Alexandra Verbovsek (eds.), *Gebauter Raum: Architektur – Landschaft – Mensch. Beiträge des fünften Münchner Arbeitskreises Junge Ägyptologie (MAJA 5), 12.12. bis 14.12.2014* (Harrasowitz: Wiesbaden).

Sansi, Roger. 2013. 'Encountering images in Candomblé', *Visual Anthropology*, 26: 18–33.

Schmitz, Bettina. 2006. 'Schönheit im alten Ägypten: Sehnsucht nach Vollkommenheit. Grundzüge des Ausstellungskonzept', in Katja Lembke and Bettina Schmitz (eds.), *Schönheit im alten Ägypten: Sehnsucht nach Vollkommenheit* (Gerstenberg: Hildesheim).

Schulz, Regine. 1992. *Die Entwicklung und Bedeutung des kuboiden Statuentypus: Eine Untersuchung zu den sogenannten "Würfelhockern"* (Gerstenberg: Hildesheim).

2011. 'Block statue', in Willeke Wendrich (ed.), *UCLA Encyclopedia of Egyptology* (eScholarship.org: Los Angeles).

Semat-Nicoud, Aude. 2013. 'L'idée du beau en Égypte ancienne', *Les dossiers d'Archéologie, hors-série spécial*, 1: 32–7.

Sethe, Kurt. 1926. *Die Ächtung feindlicher Fürsten, Völker und Dinge auf altägyptischen Tongefässcherben des Mittleren Reiches nach den Originalen im Berliner Museum* (Verlag der Akademie der Wissenschaften: Berlin).

1928. *Aegyptische Lesestücke zum Gebrauch im akademischen Unterricht* (J. C. Hinrichs'sche Buchhandlung: Leipzig).

Silverman, David (ed.). 2003. *Ancient Egypt* (Oxford University Press: Oxford and New York).

Simondon, Gilbert. 1964. *L'individu et sa genèse physico-biologique* (Presses Universitaires de France: Paris).

Sist, Loredana. 2016. 'The use of color in Egyptian statuary', in Valérie Angenot and Francesco Tiradritti (eds.), *Artists and colour in ancient Egypt: Proceedings of the colloquium held in Montepulciano, August 22nd–24th, 2008* (Missione Archeologica Italiana a Luxor: Montepulciano).

Spalinger, Anthony J. 1985. 'A redistributive pattern at Assiut', *Journal of the American Oriental Society*, 105: 7–20.

Spanel, Donald. 1988. *Through ancient eyes: Egyptian portraiture. An exhibition organized for the Birmingham Museum of Art, Birmingham Alabama* (Birmingham Museum of Art: Birmingham, AL).

Spiegelberg, Wilhelm. 1917. 'Varia', *Zeitschrift für Ägyptische Sprache und Altertumskunde*, 53: 91–115.

Stauder, Andréas. 2018. 'Staging restricted knowledge: The sculptor Irtysen's self-presentation (ca. 2000 BC)', in Gianluca Miniaci, Juan Carlos

Moreno García, Stephen Quirke, and Andréas Stauder (eds.), *The arts of making in ancient Egypt: Voices, images, and object of material producers 2000–1550 BCE* (Sidestone Press: Leiden).

Stock, Hanns. 1951. *Nṯr nfr = der gute Gott?* (Gerstenberg: Hildesheim).

Strandberg, Åsa. 2009. *The gazelle in ancient Egyptian art: Image and meaning* (Uppsala Universitet: Uppsala).

Strauss, Elisabeth-Christine. 1974. *Die Nunschale: Eine Gefässgruppe des Neuen Reiches* (Deutscher Kunstverlag: Munich).

Strudwick, Nigel C. 2005. *Texts from the Pyramid Age* (Brill: Leiden and Boston).

Sweeney, Deborah. 2004. 'Forever young? The representation of older and ageing women in ancient Egyptian art', *Journal of the American Research Center in Egypt*, 41: 67–84.

Tefnin, Roland. 1984. 'Discours et iconicité dans l'art égyptien', *Göttinger Miszellen*, 79: 55–69.

Theis, Christoffer. 2014. *Magie und Raum: Der magische Schutz ausgewählter Räume im Alten Ägypten nebst einem Vergleich zu angrenzenden Kulturbereichen* (Mohr Siebeck: Leiden).

Tillier, Anaïs. 2011. 'À propos de *nṯr nfr* comme épithète divine: Contribution à l'étude d'Osiris-Roi au Moyen Empire', *Revue d'Égyptologie*, 62: 159–74.

Tschorn, Sabine 2017. 'Nun-Schalen aus der Stadt des Neuen Reiches auf der Insel Sai', *Ägypten und Levante*, 27: 431–46.

Verbovsek, Alexandra. 2005. '"Imago Aegyptia": Wirkungsstrukturen der altägyptischen Bildsprache und ihre Rezeption. Ein programmatischer Ausblick', *Imago Aegyptia*, 1: 145–55.

2011. 'Reception and perception', in Melinda Hartwig (ed.), *A companion to ancient Egyptian art* (Wiley Blackwell: Chichester).

Vergnieux, Robert. 1999. *Recherches sur les monuments Thébains d'Amenhotep IV à l'aide d'outils informatiques* (Société d'Égyptologie: Geneva).

Vernant, Jean-Pierre. 1991. *Mortals and immortals: Collected essays* (Princeton University Press: Princeton).

Vila, André. 1973. 'Un rituel d'envoûtement au Moyen Empire égyptien', in Marc Sauter (ed.), *L'homme hier et aujourd'hui: Recueil d'études en hommage de André Leroi-Gourhan* (Éditions Cujas: Paris).

Viveiros de Castro, Eduardo. 2015. *The relative native: Essays on indigenous conceptual worlds* (HAU Books: Chicago).

Walsem, René van. 1982. 'The god Monthu and Deir el-Medîna', in R. J. Demarée and Jac J. Janssen (eds.), *Gleanings from Deir el-Medîna* (Neederlands Instituut voor het Nabije Oosten: Leiden).

2005. *Iconography of Old Kingdom elite tombs: Analysis & interpretation, theoretical and methodological aspects* (Ex Oriente Lux and Uitgiverij Peeters: Leiden, Leuven and Dudley, MA).

Waraksa, Elizabeth. 2008. 'Female figurines (pharaonic period)', in Willeke Wendrich (ed.), *UCLA Encyclopedia of Egyptology* (eScholarship: Los Angeles).

2009. *Female figurines from the Mut Precinct: Context and ritual function* (Academic Press and Vandenhoeck & Ruprecht: Fribourg and Göttingen).

Weiss, Lara. 2015. *Religious practice at Deir el-Medina* (Peeters and Nederlands Instituut voor het Nabije Oosten: Leuven and Leiden).

Wengrow, David. 2014. *The origin of monsters: Image and cognition in the first age of mechanical reproduction* (Princeton University Press: Princeton and Oxford).

Westendorf, Wolfhart. 1973. 'Zur Entstehung übertragener und abstrakter Begriffe', *Göttinger Miszellen*, 6: 135–44.

Widmaier, Kai. 2017. *Ägyptische Bilder und ägyptologische Kunst: Vorarbeiten für eine bildwissenschaftliche Ägyptologie* (Brill: Leiden and Boston).

Wilkinson, Richard H. 1994. *Symbol & magic in ancient Egyptian art* (Thames and Hudson: London and New York).

Willems, Harco. 1988. *Chests of life: A study of the typology and conceptual development of Middle Kingdom, Standard Class coffins* (Ex Oriente Lux: Leiden).

Wilson, Penelope. 2005. 'Naming names and shifting identities in ancient Egyptian iconoclasm', in Anne McClanan and Jeffrey Johnson (eds.), *Negating the image: Case studies in iconoclasm* (Ashgate: Aldershott).

Winter, Irene J. 2002. 'Defining "aesthetics" for non-Western studies: The case of ancient Mesopotamia', in Michael Ann Holly and Keith Moxey (eds.), *Art history, aesthetics, visual studies* (Sterling and Francine Clark Art Institute: Williamstown).

Žabkar, Louis V. 1968. *A study of the ba concept in ancient Egyptian texts* (University of Chicago Press: Chicago).

Zago, Silvia. 2018. 'Imagining the beyond: The conceptualization of Duat between the Old and the Middle Kingdoms ', *Journal of the American Research Center in Egypt*, 54: 203–17.

Acknowledgements

The idea of a brief introduction to ancient Egyptian conceptions and experiences of images in dialogue with recent developments in neighbouring fields first began to take form during the summer of 2018, as I was preparing my first semester of teaching in the Art History Department at Emory University. Serendipitously, the editors of the new series of Cambridge Elements, *Ancient Egypt in Context*, contacted me only a few months later with a kind invitation to contribute to the series, turning the realization of those plans into a much more concrete matter.

This Element draws on ideas developed in my research and teaching over a number of years, especially my graduate lectures in ancient Egyptian material culture at the University of Cambridge, 2014–16, as well as my undergraduate classes and graduate seminars at Emory University since 2018. I am particularly grateful to the participants in my fall 2019 graduate seminar on *Ancient Egyptian Conceptions and Experiences of Images*, Brooke Luokkala, Veronica Paltaratskaya, Claire Seidler, Emily Whitehead, and Alexandra Zigomalas, for their thoughtful engagement with questions arising directly from my work on this Element. I owe a special debt of gratitude to Prof. Gay Robins for reading and discussing a draft of the manuscript, generously offering a number of insightful ideas and suggestions.

Last, but my no means least, I want to thank my wife, Henrijette Vex Nyord, not only for her careful and enthusiastic reading of the manuscript and for producing the line drawings for the Element, but also for her unwavering support and encouragement throughout the project. It is to her that I dedicate this volume.

To Henrijette

Cambridge Elements ☰

Ancient Egypt in Context

Gianluca Miniaci
University of Pisa

Gianluca Miniaci is Senior Researcher in Egyptology at the University of Pisa, Honorary Researcher at the Institute of Archaeology, UCL – London, and Chercheur associé at the École Pratique des Hautes Études, Paris. He is currently co-director of the archaeological mission at Zawyet Sultan (Menya, Egypt). His main research interest focuses on the social history and the dynamics of material culture in the Middle Bronze Age Egypt and its interconnections between the Levant, Aegean, and Nubia.

Juan Carlos Moreno García
CNRS, Paris

Juan Carlos Moreno García (PhD in Egyptology, 1995) is a CNRS senior researcher at the University of Paris IV-Sorbonne, as well as lecturer on social and economic history of ancient Egypt at the École des Hautes Études en Sciences Sociales (EHESS) in Paris. He has published extensively on the administration, socio-economic history, and landscape organization of ancient Egypt, usually in a comparative perspective with other civilizations of the ancient world, and has organized several conferences on these topics.

Anna Stevens
University of Cambridge and Monash University

Anna Stevens is a research archaeologist with a particular interest in how material culture and urban space can shed light on the lives of the non-elite in ancient Egypt. She is Senior Research Associate at the McDonald Institute for Archaeological Research and Assistant Director of the Amarna Project (both University of Cambridge).

About the Series

The aim of this Elements series is to offer authoritative but accessible overviews of foundational and emerging topics in the study of ancient Egypt, along with comparative analyses, translated into a language comprehensible to non-specialists. Its authors will take a step back and connect ancient Egypt to the world around, bringing ancient Egypt to the attention of the broader humanities community and leading Egyptology in new directions.

Cambridge Elements ☰

Ancient Egypt in Context

Elements in the Series

Printed in the United States
By Bookmasters